Brace Yourself

for
perfect Tennis

David *by* W. Olson

authorHOUSE®

AuthorHouse™
1663 Liberty Drive
Bloomington, IN 47403
www.authorhouse.com
Phone: 1-800-839-8640

Published by AuthorHouse   10/03/2016

ISBN: 978-1-4918-5514-0 (sc)
ISBN: 978-1-4918-5515-7 (e)

Library of Congress Control Number: 2014901230

Print information available on the last page.

Contents

DEDICATED TO:
Advancing tennis, the greatest sport in the world.
Helping people learn quicker, improve faster, and play better.
Making the game more fun and popular.

A SPECIAL THANKS TO:
My wife Anita, who believed in me and my strange new swing.
And my brother Terry, the human backboard,
who helped me reach my full potential.

Moment of Truth

Tennis is a global phenomenon. What other sport has such a colorful history? It probably began as an obscure diversion, with scant rules, when bored fourteenth century French aristocrats constructed leather balls stuffed with hair and batted them back and forth with their bare hands outside the palace walls . . . game of the hand. During winters and sieges, the game would move indoors. Thankfully, their royal boredom produced something beneficial. Sadly, they eventually brought upon themselves the French Revolution. The sport survived in several countries and mutated to Sphairistike, a hybrid developed by Britain's Major Winfield in 1873. It was dubbed, Sticky.

Eventually, crude hitting instruments, nets, boundaries, and rules were adopted. Tennis rapidly gained structure and popularity. It underwent amazing changes and made mega-celebrities out of a talented elite. Now, it is almost as widespread and accessible as soccer and supported by dozens of industries. Hopefully, the sport's future holds promise of sustained growth and success. I'd love to see my innovative technique become the catalyst for our arrival at that next destination and beyond, a new paradigm. I see a tennis world of instant learning, rapid improvement, and pure joy.

Since the past is the key to the future, let me share a slice of my past to explain how I acquired the technique that I hope will add something helpful to the vast ocean of tennis knowledge which owes its existence to countless contributors throughout the last five centuries.

Like most intense events, there is something about the moment of discovery that rivets it in the mind for life. My special event was on a typical, muggy July evening in Minnesota, back in 1979. That is when I accidentally discovered the Brace. Or, I should say, when it discovered me.

Frankly, nothing in this world is absolutely original. It's all there already, like Michelangelo's sculpture of David hidden inside a block of marble. It just hasn't revealed itself until a certain person in a long chain of searchers just happens to go one step farther than those who preceded him, and from whom he learned everything he knows. As Isaac Newton acknowledged, "If I have seen farther than other men, it is by standing on the shoulders of giants."

No, I'm not calling myself the Newton of tennis, but I share the sense of modest gratitude he felt toward those who preceded and taught him. For me, the motivation to search was my vain attempt to defeat my father, Bucky Olson, at the game he had easily mastered at a young age. Since he would typically hit everything to my backhand, I knew there was only one solution to my dilemma.

I desperately sought the perfect backhand swing. Who doesn't? If necessity is the mother of invention, passion is the father. Mediocre with one hand and dissatisfied with the two—hander (both hands on the racquet handle), I must have looked ridiculous standing in front of my full length mirror in my cramped apartment, swinging my tennis racquet, after having moved the fragile living room furniture out of the way to appease my concerned wife. I was more concerned with protecting my new graphite racquets from damage.

Swinging-swinging-swinging . . . at times I became confused and frustrated. The threshold of discovery is often filled with despairing moments, beckoning one to retreat from continued pursuit and eventual success. Bruce Lee once said that a man fails only when he gives up. I also admire Thomas Edison . . . 9,999 failures in search of a working light bulb. Without motivation from within, one is easily tempted to give up. It's as if Destiny always tests the determination of those who seek her hidden treasures of innovation and invention.

Several nights of determined swinging and analyzing paid off at an unexpected moment when, during one particularly forceful swing with two hands, my left hand (I'm right handed) accidentally slipped off the racquet handle and onto my perspiration-soaked right arm. I froze that pose in the 'follow through' position. It felt strange, but somehow right.

"That's it!" I shouted to the startled and amazed reflection in the mirror before me.

The realization that something so momentous could occur so suddenly was overwhelming. My heart pounded. My body began to perspire nervously and my hands quivered with excitement. The adrenaline flow was incredible.

My wife called from her sewing machine in the other room. "What is?"

I ran in and showed her what I had stumbled upon just then.

"That's completely new, isn't it?" she remarked. And she didn't even play tennis!

"It sure is," I exhaled nervously. "It's a simple change, but it could make a huge difference. I can't wait to test it on the court."

Returning to the mirror, I continued demonstrating this strange and curious novelty to make sure it was a genuine improvement. New, yes. But beneficial? At first it seemed uncomfortably different and awkward. I wanted to sit and record my new sensations, but I kept a tight grip on my wrist, afraid that if I were to let go, somehow I would forget how to reproduce this new swing correctly and it would be lost forever. Silly, I know. Or worse, I'd wake up from a dream to my old, boring, ineffective backhand, the one Bucky enjoyed tormenting.

The more I practiced, the more comfortable this new swing began to feel. I looked up and saw a strange image in the mirror. Is this real? Why doesn't anybody use this? Why hasn't anybody ever tried this? Am I wasting my time? My mind raced as I felt this new swing dramatically alter my mediocre one hand style. I searched for paper and pencil, finally tearing my hand off my forearm, hands still trembling from the thrilling experience. I quickly recorded thoughts and observations, fearing they would be lost if not immediately captured in writing.

As I glanced up to ponder the improvements, my reflection gazed at me with that smug smile, the one that says, "I know something nobody else does."

But that smile was also one of anticipation and awe. I knew this helpful technique would one day conquer and change the world. Oh, it might take a while, but eventually it would transform the game of tennis and become the orthodox stroke worldwide. I believed it. I knew it.

Beginners using this method would learn more easily. Average players, frustrated at their lack of progress and aptitude, would improve quickly with less effort. But most of all, everyone's enjoyment of tennis would skyrocket. These sublime thoughts raced through my mind while I faced that smiling, sweaty image in the mirror at that moment of discovery.

In this book, we will discuss a new technique (Brace) and how it adapts to and improves two strokes (groundstroke and volley) on two different sides (forehand and backhand). Let's define the strokes now to avoid any confusion for the beginner, or anyone who plays but doesn't care about the lingo.

A groundstroke is a ball you strike after it bounces once (twice for wheelchair rules). A volley is a ball hit in midair after it crosses the net but before it bounces. (Never volley a ball if you are certain it will bounce outside the lines.) A half volley is a misnomer. It actually bounces immediately before you hit it near the ground. It should be called a half-groundie, but that is neither here nor there. Groundstrokes and volleys are similar swings. Forehands and Backhands are different, but not quite as different as pens and aardvarks. That too is neither here nor there. They're more like pens and pencils.

Chapter One

Backhand Groundstroke

It's not your racquet
It's not your string.
The secret to tennis
Is in your swing!

A perfect backhand? Unless you're a professional it sounds impossible, doesn't it? Most of us are happy just slapping, chopping, or blocking the ball back over the net defensively, resigning ourselves to possessing a functional, but mediocre, backhand. A one-handed backhand has good reach and versatility (ability to volley, for instance), but it often lacks power, control, and consistency. A two-handed backhand adds power and consistency, but can't be used to volley or hit with slice, besides other disadvantages.

With the Brace technique providing perfect form and more than double the strength of one arm, you'll soon look forward to blasting even first serves back for winners. In fact, your confidence will build so much that when the ball comes right at you, your new tendency will be to take a quick step to your right and use your flawless 'Braced' backhand. In fact, you may even find yourself running around your decent forehand to hit your bread-and-butter backhand. That is, until you master the Brace forehand, then both sides will be equally effective and high-confidence shots. You'll then have the pleasant problem of deciding between two equally excellent options.

How can the Brace be more than twice as strong as the one-handed backhand? The average person's straight arm can lift about 20 pounds sideways, in the motion imitating the backhand follow through. It's no surprise, since only the sparse shoulder muscles are involved in lifting an extended straight arm, which itself weighs almost that much. (Only when your own arm falls asleep, do you discover its true weight.)

But with the Brace hand adding support about midway between hand and elbow and utilizing the triceps and bicep muscles of that assisting arm, the leverage strength increases to more than 50 pounds. Imagine all that power transferred into the ball. Obviously, the two-handed backhand is popular because of this same harnessed power. But power is not the only factor involved. Reach, freedom, versatility, control, and comfort are added to the long list of advantages the Brace brings . . . things which the two-hander can't deliver.

If you use one hand to hit the backhand, you gain and you lose. The same principle applies if you use two hands for your backhand. Each is unique, with a unique set of pros and cons. Let's examine each one, then proceed to the innovative technique that has no drawbacks.

With one hand you have better reach for low or high balls. You also have versatility, or variety of shot selection, and the option of a better transition to the net because you already have experience and wrist strength from using one hand. Basically, your wrist is free to flex, adjust angles, and dominate the racquet. You also have more reach on service returns and stretching for wide shots. You can slice, drive or hit with topspin. So what can go wrong? Plenty. You might not have the power or racquet speed you need for a good swing, especially off balance or on the run. Plus, it takes longer to accelerate your racquet and time the impact with the ball. With a long one-handed swing, the tendency is to hit late on a ball coming at you quickly. It's plain physics. If a shot forces you to hit on the run, you might get to it, but not be able to do much with it. Ironically, in those situations, weight shift and shoulder action are more crucial to compensate for less upper body strength. If you try to increase power too much, you can lose consistency and control and risk bending your swing too much. We're forced to use only our arm much of the time. Face it, the power on that side of the body is not abundant. But all in all, you can develop a good range of shots, as long as you have time to hit them and your opponent misses eventually from your defensive strategy. So, the drawbacks are only obvious against a consistent and powerful player. Most of your opponents will be one or the other. Not encouraging.

Two hands is a viable and popular alternative . . . and the only one at present. You can't argue with success. It has anchored itself as the preferred choice of most players, especially beginners, children, and many women . . . with good reason. It's just a matter of muscle mass. I intend to reverse that trend. If you develop a decent two-hander, you gain control, consistency and power. Your stroke becomes more mechanical . . . robotic, if you will. That's not bad, unless your opponent finds one of the several weaknesses in your stroke, like that special spin shot that drives you crazy because your two-hander cannot handle it well. Or wide balls that you have to run for. You must take extra steps to reach the ball, compared to the one-hander. Or it may be a certain height of bounce that is your weakness. And what's more, you cannot hit a slice. You can hit hard, but the flaws are revealed with the style. Your volley might not be great, not only because your wrist is weaker from lack of use at the baseline (for many players, 'net' is a 4 letter word), but also from the timing change that ensues when switching from two to one.

Face it, when you drop one hand off the grip, the racquet becomes twice as heavy. You may not be used to the change. One hand or two is not a case of choosing the lesser of two evils, but settling for the best personal option of two average equals. I know. I tried both styles for years. Both deliver what they were designed to deliver. But they both fall short of delivering the best possible combination of benefits. Let's see how the Brace becomes all things to all players . . . how you hold and use the Brace and with what advantages.

The hand holding the racquet will be referred to as the right hand or right arm or right wrist. Left handed players need only reverse the photographs and terms to follow the instructions. I don't like playing lefties, so I will get my revenge here by ignoring them. They should be banned from tennis. I hope none of them ever use the Brace and defeat me with it. I'm only kidding. I hope they all try it and love it. I'm not afraid of them, even with the Brace. I have a secret strategy for beating them that I won't reveal in this book. I'll take that one to the grave. They should be forced to wear an identifying badge, though, like a giant scarlet

'L' on their chest. I've had experiences before where I didn't noticed they were lefties until halfway into the first set! Talk about a Homer Simpson moment. No wonder their backhands were so good.

Place your left hand on top of your right forearm, halfway between your hand and your elbow, just above your wrist, where the thinner tendons connect to and transition to muscle. Your palm rests on the inside of your forearm, your fingers overlap the outside. Your thumb rests alongside your index finger, not opposite the fingers. Grasping the forearm with the opposing thumb creates a right angle with the right wrist and lifts your left elbow. Pretend your thumb and index finger are webbed or glued together and pointing in the same direction. You can experiment with the advanced grip with the thumb under your forearm after you become more advanced. Start with the first hold shown in **Photograph A**.

Photograph N shows the alternative Wrist-Wrap Brace . . . similar benefits but with a different feel and set of muscles involved. Each person should decide which type adapts best to his or her own style and technique. Most players who use one hand will gravitate to the L-Bow Brace (**Photograph A**). Players who use two hands will generally find the Wrist-Wrap Brace more comfortable and compatible (**Photograph N**). It's more similar to what you have been using, hence an easier transition.

Both types work for groundstrokes and volleys on both sides, but they have slightly different characteristics and strengths, which even I am still discovering. (The Wrist-Wrap might be slightly better at hitting a topspin while the L-Bow Brace hits a more perfect slice. But both Braces hit both shots well. You can probably guess what combination I now use.) So my advice is to pick one that works best for you, then master it. Don't worry about rushing to decide. They are both interchangeable. Take your time. You might even become one of those rare people who switch back and forth depending on the situation. It's apples and oranges. It's not like switching from the archaic one-hander to two. The L-Bow and Wrist-Wrap are almost identical in many ways. This is your choice between two great equals. The success will depend on how proficient you can become with the particular Brace you choose and work diligently with. (See Advanced Brace Theory section.)

This L-Bow hold on your forearm may remind you of the game you might have played with your friends when you were very young. You and a partner constructed a human chair by assuming the similar arm positions shown in Photograph A. Then the two of you locked hands to opposite arms, forming a strong square with all four arms to carry a third seated person. Pretty sturdy 'Braced' chair, is it not?

Adjust the location of your left hand upon the right forearm to find the most comfortable spot for you personally. Arm length, hand size, and even girth (wrist, not waist) may determine different locations where your arm will rest most comfortably. Remember that the slightest change in position of the Brace on the right forearm affects the swing in different ways. It's called leverage. I will explain later.

With the Brace hooked up, your forearms make the letter 'L,' and your left hand holds on between your wrist and your elbow . . . hence the name of this hold is the L-Bow Brace. Depending on the effects (leverage, acceleration, control, etc.) on your swing that you desire, the Brace can be closer to the wrist than the elbow, or vice versa. This Brace is one of three possible types, but it is the easiest and most versatile for all strokes. Therefore, it is the easiest Brace to learn first and the ideal one to start using exclusively.

I recommend the Eastern Backhand grip. It's the best one to use with this Brace, since it can be used, not only for hitting sliced groundstrokes on both wings, but also for volleying on both sides. For volleying, I use what I call an 'East-inental' grip. It's midway between an Eastern backhand and the Continental. Two-handers may need to get used to a new grip if they were using the Eastern or even Western forehand grip with the right hand. The object of the backhand grip is essentially for the hand to get positioned behind the racquet and push it (like a flat wall) through the ball. A French pro named Francois Durr was a unique exception when she found a way to use the forehand grip and an extended index finger, essentially pulling the racquet through her backhand swing with a bent wrist (and a very strong wrist it was). It is rarely tried, or recommended, today. Turn your racquet grip clockwise (to the right) in your hand until the racquet face is perpendicular (straight up and down) to the ground when you hold it at your side.

When time allows, switch to the Eastern forehand grip, the 'shake hands' grip, when hitting the topspin forehand. You may prefer the Western grip on forehand groundstrokes. Either way, always switch back to the Eastern or Continental backhand grip after hitting a topspin forehand. This is because you can hit a decent forehand slice groundstroke with any backhand grip, but you can't hit a decent backhand with either forehand grip. This is one reason why I volley and return serves with a backhand grip. When there is no time to change grips, simply bend the wrist back slightly and hit a slice forehand, as you would a volley. Now, let's get back to the Brace backhand stroke.

The Brace backhand groundstroke is divided into three simple phases, all part of one smooth swing. The first part is the backswing. As soon as the ball crosses the net and you realize you must hit a backhand (and your heart skips a beat), the Brace hand exerts pulling pressure on your right arm, automatically twisting your shoulders and trunk to your left side.

(See Photograph B)

Notice how the upper body actually initiates the backswing motion, then the feet follow, not the other way around. This is the first advantage experienced by the action of the Brace upon the right forearm. Your shoulders are automatically turned sideways by this pulling action on your right arm. Your right arm also stays low during the first phase of the backswing, due to the natural weight of the Brace hand upon it. Its intended direction is around the body instead of up. That would waste precious time you don't have. Your right arm is straight and low . . . straight because the elbow is kept close to the body, low because the hitting arm is kept straight, unless you desire more racquet speed. In that case, you can lift both Brace and hitting forearm above your shoulder after the first phase of the backswing is complete, only if the ball is hit slowly enough to allow time for this. Extra momentum should ideally come from straightening the legs, shifting your weight and uncoiling your shoulders slightly.

Whatever unique racquet position you prefer, you can feel it in that position because you are holding it there. It's not floating around by your head or wrapped around your neck without your knowledge. This happens often to one-handers. They may think their racquet is low when it isn't. You'll always control it and be aware of its location because your left hand is resting upon your right wrist, sensing, detecting and directing its movement in both directions.

Don't set the racquet in a vertical position. This will cause too much wrist action when you try to swoop under the ball while swinging. Keep the angle between the racquet and wrist more than 90 degrees. This is not racquetball, it's tennis. It's preferable to build racquet speed with a longer backswing than a higher one. Or flatten and wrap the racquet behind your back for more racquet speed. But those angles and swings are style choices and my advice on this is mere suggestion so you can make the most of the potential that the Brace provides. The rest is window dressing. Keep it simple and consistent. The power is already guaranteed without extraneous tricks.

This backswing may not feel comfortable at first try because it is the complete and proper backswing, not a partial one with just the forearm and not the shoulders. The Brace may stretch you farther than you may have been used to, even with a two-hander. Some backswings are halfway, with the elbow and body almost facing the net and the arm and racquet wrapped around the body, ready to slowly uncoil into a half-swing that ends when the forearm catches up to the elbow and stops when the arm is straight. In this volume I am not going to dwell on many fine points of tennis technique. There are plenty of those already. I will concentrate on how my new method helps you play better along with a few universal fundamentals.

The pulling action of the Brace causes an immediate and full backswing, allowing time to set up for the stroke and meet the ball in front. The last second backswing hitch often results in that rushed and incomplete stroke. Old habits are hard to break, but not with the Brace. The backswing becomes one motion, swift and complete, with the pause after it is completed instead of in the middle of the swing. I like to pull the racquet a bit farther back just before contact, just to create extra momentum . . . but only after a complete preparation. It's not a hitch in the true sense. It only allows me to follow the ball all the way to the racquet.

A two-hander will find this backswing similar, yet more comfortable, with the left arm bent and ready to begin the forward swing. For two-handers, I usually recommend the Wrist Wrap Brace (**Photograph N**) instead of the less constrictive L-Bow. It is more similar to their former style. Same grip, except that the left hand holds the wrist instead of the racquet handle. The fingers are under the forearm and the thumb is on top, mimicking the grip formerly used on the racquet handle. It allows the option of holding on to the forearm during the entire swing and encourages more shoulder rotation, a trademark of the two-hander. It's basically a two-handed clone on steroids. My other manual uses photos with this method. It's called "Brace Method for Tennis." It shows only the Wrist Wrap Brace for the backhand. The only differences are the fingers and the follow through. The advantages are identical.

A brief word about footwork. The Brace can prod and assist the feet to form a closed stance, but not force them. That is under your control. A closed stance means that the front foot is closer to the net and the sideline than the back, or left, foot. This position allows the hips and shoulders to rotate freely during the backswing. It is crucial that the feet not hinder shoulder and hip rotation. Otherwise, a complete backswing is impossible, even with the Brace. At least get the right foot out in front if your body. An open stance backhand is okay in emergencies, but should not become a habit.

The contact zone is the second part of the backhand stroke. (**See Photograph C**)

Between backswing and contact, the Brace pushes the racquet arm forward and up, accelerating the racquet toward contact. The weight shifts from the back foot to the front. That combination of body weight and arm action is tremendous.

I can't stress this enough . . . Keep a firm wrist. One way to do this is by squeezing the grip tighter than you would on the forehand side. Let your hands and arms learn to work together as a team. The timing takes getting used to, because with one hand it took more time to get the racquet moving. Now, though, you will be able to swing much faster when the ball arrives, avoiding late hits forever. Early hits and a floppy wrist might be your first encounter. Counter them both by swinging smoothly and even gently, until your timing and confidence improves.

The Brace exerts pressure on the lower forearm, preventing the elbow from bending or leading the stroke. The elbow is kept close to the body and the arm is kept straight. The racquet hand catches up to and passes the elbow at contact. The Brace reinforces the right forearm at contact, allowing you to hit through the ball solidly. The slight pressure on your right arm at the beginning of your swing reminds you to keep your wrist firm. However, if you exert too much pressure above your wrist before you are accustomed to the altered timing, you might get a floppy racquet coming through the contact zone instead of a smooth, solid perpendicular wall. Push (don't slap) the wall through the ball. Your wrist is free to bring your racquet head around and forward, adding to acceleration and firm contact with the ball.

At contact, the Brace shows its true value. The right hand is still pushing toward the net, preventing the racquet from following its natural tendency to swing around the body. The advantage over the two-handed backhand is twofold. First of all, the racquet arm is held rigid, not bent, allowing a longer and straighter contact zone. Secondly, less shoulder rotation allows more control over directional placement. Several factors determine where the ball goes, two of them being follow through and shoulder rotation. These are as important as point of contact.

Two-handers have trouble with reach on low balls and wide shots. The Brace actually improves the reach to become superior even to one hand. How? It allows more time to get to the ball because less time is needed for the actual swing. Plus, it assists the follow through to go in the desired direction. An extra hand guiding the racquet without interfering with it can control the contact zone and follow through. It's a game of inches, especially when the racquet meets the ball. So much is determined in that small space.

Neither one hand nor two hands can provide the unique extended contact zone that you experience with the Brace. The shoulder, elbow, and even wrist, are all reinforced and stabilized for a solid, smooth contact zone. The Brace lets you choose between slice, drive, and topspin. The photographs shown for the volleys can be used as a guide to what a 'Braced' slice groundstroke looks like. The slice is like the volley, just longer and more level.

The third phase of the backhand groundstroke is the follow through. **(See Photograph D)**

Placement is made easy by choosing the direction to follow through and then letting the Brace guide your right arm toward the target.

Topspin and depth are provided by the Brace as it pushes your right arm smoothly upward and out through the contact zone. After, and only after, contact should the Brace hand then gracefully let go and slow its forward movement and allow the right arm to continue up and out for a full follow through. When the arms work together, a consistent and aggressive topspin drive is possible. You have the freedom to add more wrist action, raise or lower your follow through, and use more or less shoulder rotation for disguise, spin variety, and pace changes. You can also keep holding on to your arm even after contact for a more compact swing, and added control.

Notice in the photograph that the free, or Brace, hand does not stop until impact with the ball is complete. Otherwise, it does not accomplish its purpose, to steady and strengthen the racquet during contact with the ball. If you let go too soon, the Brace cannot help you with either impact or follow through. Feel both hands move through the ball and finish the swing. Whether you hit down the line or crosscourt, the Brace travels the same distance . . . past the contact zone.

The backhand groundstroke Brace formula: **Pull down/Push up**.

(This phrase is from the perspective of what action the Brace is performing in cooperation with your hitting arm during a drive or topspin stroke, even though it goes without saying that the Brace assists the swing, but doesn't do all the work. A more technically accurate phrase might be: Guide down/Guide up.)

Each swing and every ball you hit is different. That goes for tennis, generally. If you hit a slice groundstroke, the formula changes to Pull (or guide) up/Push (or guide) down. The Brace may do more during the backswing and less during the follow through . . . or vice versa. When it becomes second nature, it does exactly what is needed, when it's needed, for whatever shot is chosen and executed. You are still hitting the ball with your stronger arm, the one that is holding the racquet. The Brace is assisting, teaching, correcting, and perfecting. But the more you use it, the less you will be able to tell which arm is doing what. They become a synchronized team . . . a successfully fused unit. Really, your entire upper body begins operating as a hitting unit.

Photograph A . . . L-Bow Brace

Photograph B . . . Backhand Groundstroke Backswing

Photograph C . . . Backhand Groundstroke Contact Zone

Photograph D . . . Backhand Groundstroke Follow Through

Chapter Two

Backhand Volley

As if a perfect backhand groundstroke wasn't enough, it gets better. The groundstroke isn't the only shot that you can now improve, using the Brace. Your backhand volley is about to get an extreme makeover. You won't believe the difference it can make to your game and confidence.

The backhand volley, though short and smooth as a motion, is quite difficult to execute. Control is poor, due to the different heights encountered while volleying. Timing is difficult since it is done at the net with a variety of speeds and spins with which to contend. Volleys are weak for several reasons:

1) Volleys are often hit above the shoulder or at awkward angles, with the weakest muscles of the arm involved in moving the racquet. The shoulder and biceps are usually dormant.

2) Volleys are often hit late because the ball comes at you twice as fast and can be difficult to time.

3) The muscles involved on the backhand side are weaker than the forehand, especially if you do not have time to move your feet and lean into the shot.

4) I call it a shot and not a stroke, because it is much shorter than the backhand groundstroke, so there is less time to generate racquet speed, hence less power. Words like punch, jab, or block are used to describe the volley.

5) If you have a two-handed backhand, your volley muscles are going to be weaker than a person who hits all his groundstrokes with one hand. That is the unfortunate tradeoff of using two

hands. You cannot consistently and successfully use two hands to volley.

Have no fear, the Brace is here. The Brace is ideal for volleying. The backhand volley is short and quick, but it still consists of three harmonious parts. The first phase in the volley is the backswing, although it is not technically a 'swing back' compared to the groundstroke. The length of the volley is about half that of the groundstroke, the backswing being the part mostly sacrificed to save time. It's more of a hitch or pivot than a backswing, but let's keep using the same terms as the groundstroke for clarity. (**See Photograph E**)

The volley backswing is more like a shoulder turn and elbow bend, similar to preparing to throw a Frisbee.

The Brace improves the backswing several ways:

First of all, the pull on your racquet arm automatically turns your shoulders in one motion, resulting in an instant backswing. This results in a volley that is straight, toward the net, not diagonal and across the body. Some players use their free hands to achieve the same correct backswing that is pictured in **Photograph E**. The drawback is that it has to end there. The other hand cannot help past this phase of the stroke. If you keep holding on during the next phase, your forward swing will start to curve around your body and your shoulders will open too soon, cramping your forward motion.

Secondly, the backswing is short on the volley, so the Brace can be used simultaneously as a sensor, stopping the racquet hand at its proper position near the left shoulder. The Brace can prevent a long unnecessary backswing. You only have time for an abbreviated backswing. Even in the ready position, the Brace can be used to stretch your arms almost straight, bringing the racquet closer to the net. Always hold the racquet above net level when facing the net and awaiting the ball's approach, so the racquet has less distance to travel to the preferred backswing position above your shoulder.

Third, the Brace connection with the right arm allows you to feel the height of your backswing and make corrections instinctively. You always know where your racquet is, without looking, without guessing. Learn to relax and just feel what the Brace is doing for you.

16

The Brace is far superior to the two-handed backhand mainly due to its ability to adapt and be effective at improving the volley. The two-hander has difficulty adjusting from groundstroke to volley. Two hands can rarely be used for volleying because it inhibits a proper contact in front of the body, among other reasons.

The second phase of the volley is, of course, the contact point. (**See Photograph F**)

The Brace's gentle guidance during the forward push reminds you to squeeze the racquet grip, to maintain a firm wrist during impact. The Brace helps you contact the ball well in front of your body for eye contact, control, and placement. A downward angle is naturally assisted for slice, but the Brace also guides the racquet hand through the contact point at the same time. It might not be as long a contact zone as a groundstroke, but severe chopping can cause errors and weak volleys.

The Brace will surprise you with what it can do on high volleys and especially backhand overheads . . . yes, overheads! Practice will make perfect if you stick with it.

After contact with the ball, comes the third phase of the volley . . . follow through. (**See Photograph G**)

The Brace guides the racquet hand through the ball and toward the selected target, then stops, lets go of the hitting arm, and allows the racquet to continue in a natural path forward. The volley follow through is not as long as the groundstroke's counterpart, although well in front of the body. Remember that the volley backswing is far shorter than the follow through, but the entire stroke is telescoped. Basically, the volley is more of a controlled 'Tap' than a swing. Turn/Tap, I tell my students. Keep it simple.

This may seem redundant, but two hands are stronger than one. However, the two-hander per se is not feasible for the volley. The Brace upon the forearm initiates a quick shoulder turn, then guides a short, high backswing and a quick, angled Swop (cross between a swing and a chop) that starts above the shoulder (depending on the ball's height) and ends at or below the waist. It adds power without lengthening the stroke into an unpredictable swing. The ball's own speed is often used to generate all the pace needed.

After letting go of the racquet arm and finishing the volley, simply return to the ready position with the left hand on top of the right forearm. You're now ready for the next volley, if there is one. A deep or angled volley is dependent on the direction and length of your Swop.

Reminder: The fact that a volley is struck so far in front of the body and it is mainly a motion of the hands to perform, are two reasons why it can't be done well with two hands on the racquet handle. The Brace solves this dilemma by allowing sufficient reach to volley in front of the body and by reinforcing the forearm. It kills two birds with one stone. Killer volleys, too.

The Brace backhand volley formula: **Pull up/Push down**

(I might add, 'Release arm after contact,' but that is naturally accomplished. And if you want to add the risky but impressive topspin volley to your repertoire, reverse the formula to Pull down/Push up. But please, get proficient at the boring but effective slice volley first.)

Photograph E . . . Backhand Volley Backswing

Photograph F . . . Backhand Volley Contact Point

Photograph G . . . Backhand Volley Follow Through

Chapter Three

Forehand Groundstroke

Although the forehand stroke is a strength and a high confidence shot for most players, it still produces many errors and is hit using many different styles. When it comes to spins and shots available, including things that can go wrong, the possibilities seem endless. Because of the awkward stages of the swing and the various body sections used, many things can and do go wrong. In the case of a good forehand swing, one size does not fit all. But there are only a few basics from which you can build a solid foundation. Among these are weight balance, footwork, hip and shoulder rotation, and imparting topspin and power with the follow through with some or much wrist action.

Right from the start, the backswing may be too high, too late, too short, or too far away from the body. The wrist, elbow, and shoulders are three independent body parts, sometimes with minds of their own, that make the forehand stroke unpredictable and, at times, frustrating. Could there be a way to connect and control these independent joints and muscles to make them cooperate? Yes, the Brace can by transforming the upper body into a single, harmonious hitting unit. Each part of the body involved in the stroke is held and guided through its proper position and function.

Errors are few because the backswing is early, the contact zone is extended, and the follow through is complete. Power is doubled, believe it or not, not only because the full strength of the left shoulder is transferred directly into the ball, but the left arm is also pulling the racquet arm through the contact zone. The first comment from many people trying the Brace for the first time is, "I can really feel the difference."

Weight testing has measured the average forehand strength (arm only) at about 40 pounds of pressure, compared to 80 pounds with the Brace (arm and shoulders) assisting. You won't believe your eyes when you see what you can do with the Brace forehand.

You won't have to worry anymore about where your racquet is, how far your shoulders have rotated, or how straight your arm is, because the Brace will take care of all those elements of your stroke. The mechanics will be correct because the Brace will hold all the moving parts in place and guide them through the proper swing, freeing you to concentrate on the important things, like the ball and your footwork. Eliminating all the details of how to hit frees your mind to focus on the more important aspects of the stroke.

Once you have become comfortable and competent with the Brace, you may want to hold your free hand on your racquet hand at all times, switching between two grips with one hand.

Several benefits are realized with the Brace during the first stage of the forehand stroke, the backswing. **(See Photograph H)**

The key to success with the Brace forehand is the direct connection of the left, or opposite, shoulder to the hitting arm. One would assume they are already connected, but they aren't. Too many people hit the forehand with only their arm. They may assume they are using all their strength, but most of it is wasted, or dormant. The shoulders may lazily move a little back and forth during the swing, but only because they are reluctantly dragged around the body for the backswing, then pushed out of the way by the right arm as it pushes through the ball. The shoulders and hips usually operate on separate swivels, at times out of sync with your intention. Most players use only a partial shoulder turn. The shoulder/arm ratio of movement during the swing should be 50/50, an equal participation stroke. Usually it is 20/80, or at best 40/60, in favor of the arm. That puts undue pressure and stress on the arm. Believe it or not, you can also develop elbow pain from too many improper forehand groundstrokes, where the elbow is overworked.

On the backswing, racquet movement is of secondary importance to shoulder and trunk rotation. Once completed, the hands and racquet are free to loop up, back, then down, gathering speed and making solid contact with perfect timing. Timing is the key to power. The two parts of your backswing that generate power are your shoulders and your wrist. Whether you use a giant loopy swing or simply a straight back method, the end result shown in photograph H is crucial to building up the racquet speed needed to impart the spin and power during the rest of the swing.

It doesn't matter how you get from the ready position to the state shown in photograph H as long as you get there. Most teachers recommend some kind of loop, if only to assist proper timing, and to keep the racquet moving during the entire swing.

All that power and potential is usually wasted when the shoulders could be cooperating with and strengthening the arm. An instant backswing and shoulder turn is achieved when the Brace pushes on the right wrist, forcing the arm and racquet back and down. Your left shoulder follows your Brace hand. Many players can take their racquets back without turning their shoulders completely, to their dismay. The shoulders determine power and the direction of your swing, among other things. If they are only partially rotated, your swing will be pulled left, like a irritating golf slice. A helpful drill is to aim all forehands down the line. You can't do this consistently without rotating your shoulders properly. The crosscourt forehand is more natural. The down the line shot takes more care and effort. Don't limit your options with an incomplete shoulder rotation and backswing. The Brace ensures a complete backswing and better options.

You may push up with the Brace to form a loop during your backswing for better timing, or push straight back. Your wind up does not matter as long as you finish low, below the ball. Of course, the shortest distance between two points is a straight line, which is why I recommend that you try pushing down and back for the quickest possible backswing, allowing the wrist to provide the looping action. While you bring your racquet around and down, change your grip from the Eastern backhand to the Eastern forehand, the shake hands grip. Or use some form of Western for more topspin. Learn to do it with one hand.

With the backswing complete, the feet have moved their position to follow the hips and shoulders. An open stance is popular and occasionally necessary, but its drawback is that it hinders the shoulder turn. With the

Brace you can have your cake and eat it too. The torso will start acting independently of the legs. As long as you keep your knees bent and feet far apart, your shoulders and hips will rotate freely.

The wrist is always bent back for firmness and to impart topspin. The racquet head can be lowered for imparting extra topspin and racquet speed. Some of these adjustments are details of style that the Brace allows for and does not hamper. As is true for the backhand, the wrist on the forehand side is allowed freedom of movement. The bad habits are eliminated, the good ones are enhanced and encouraged . . . maybe even forced upon you.

Like snowflakes, no two swings are identical. I'm sure most physicists will agree with me. Hundreds of factors are involved in each bounce of the ball and movement of the racquet. This is especially true of the backswing. Some players take the racquet straight back, some loop it in various ways. Some lead with their elbow, some with their hand. The point is, it's not how you get there that matters, it's that you achieve the correct result. Your shoulders rotate, your wrist bends back, and the racquet gets below the ball. The Brace assists with all three things.

The contact zone follows the backswing as the crucial second phase of the forehand swing. **(See Photograph I)**

The hips and shoulders have rotated first, triggering the whip-like transfer of power into the left arm, which the Brace, in turn, directly applies to the hitting arm, wrist and racquet. There is neither delay nor wasted energy. The racquet accelerates up and into the ball, ideally meeting it somewhere between the belly button and left hip (I'm referring to contact point and not height) and at least a racquet's length away from the body. Think of pulling the racquet through the swing with the hips and shoulders, rather than pushing it with the arms. The opposite is true for the backhand, which is mainly an action of the legs and arms getting behind the racquet and lifting, then pushing it into the ball like a wall . . . hence the forehand's power advantage. More muscle power using bigger muscles.

The Brace holds the right elbow close to the body, preventing it from interfering with the stroke. The wrist is kept relaxed and bent back at contact and allowed freedom to adjust to different ball speeds and spins, and last second changes. The Brace provides full reach and power, the force of two hands, the feel of one. Most players use wrist action, some don't.

The extended contact zone will provide control over the ball. It will also lift the ball over the net and impart topspin to keep it in the court. The Brace also prevents errors from occurring during impact, when so many things can go wrong. After contact is made, the stroke is not finished. So much success depends on a good finish. Depth and placement are determined by the length and direction of the follow through, the key to a good forehand. (**See Photograph J**)

The Brace improves both. It guides the hitting arm up and through the ball, finishing in front of the right shoulder for placement down the line, or nearer the left shoulder for a placement crosscourt. Both arms end the follow through bent to add natural topspin and depth.

The Brace literally forces you to 'hit out,' by creating a full follow through. It adds power by rotating the shoulders and accelerating the racquet even after contact. The natural tendency often is to end, or at least slow down, the swing at contact, causing the ball to fly out of court or into the net. That added stretch toward the net is the key to control and consistency.

By pulling on the racquet arm, the Brace also pulls the right shoulder forward to finish under the chin, allowing the fullest possible extension of the stroke. If the shoulders do not rotate the hitting arm is hindered and wraps around the body and cannot reach out toward the net, sacrificing depth, pace, and power.

Unlike the backhand follow through, there is no need to let go of the Brace during the forehand follow through because the forehand swing ends closer to the body than the backhand. Simply resume the ready position after the follow through.

The highly simplified formula for the forehand groundstroke: **Push down/Pull up**.

Final Forehand Thoughts

I can't stress this enough. Keep the Brace relaxed. It should act like a flexible steel cable connecting the hitting arm to the left shoulder, not a steel rod. You'll find out what I mean as you practice with it. If you tense or stiffen up, the arm and shoulders will be out of sync. A relaxed and loose forehand is a more powerful forehand. Get the wrist bent back as soon as possible. Otherwise it might not be bent at contact. You might have or want some kind of loop in your backswing, not shown in the photo that would have preceded photograph H, which only depicts where you want the racquet to be immediately before the forward swing begins. How you get to this point is up to your individual style and the speed/height/spin of the ball that is hit at you. I could have inserted several photos depicting the circular route from the ready position to backswing. But that would have distracted you from the main point. Get there any way you want, as long as you get ready correctly and on time. Many players slow down their forehand backswings to keep momentum going until the forward swing. Whatever works for you, works for me. The Brace can accommodate diverse styles. The shoulders lead the backswing, then they lead the forward swing. Backswing height and movement are usually irrelevant, as long as it improves your timing. If you have a big swing with a big loop, your formula would be some kind of hybrid like, Push up-back-down/Pull up.

Photograph H . . . Forehand Groundstroke Backswing

Photograph I . . . Forehand Groundstroke Contact Zone

Photograph J . . . Forehand Groundstroke Follow Through

Chapter Four

Forehand Volley

Although the forehand volley looks simple and easy, there is much room for improvement. Most people learn and develop a decent forehand volley quickly. As a stroke, it doesn't get much attention from the average player. They may assume it is a simple stroke to master. The serve and the backhand are the focus of most people looking for advanced instruction.

Like the corresponding groundstroke, there are many body parts involved in the shot. The Brace provides better form automatically. It unites the body parts involved into a graceful unit and guides each component during the shot. Because of where the hitting arm is positioned on the forehand side, the volley backswing is easy . . . almost too easy. Often, the shoulders don't turn as they should, since by simply sticking your right arm sideways, your backswing is practically ready. However, the reason the shoulders must turn for the volley backswing is the same reason they must turn for the forehand groundstroke. Otherwise, the arm will have a natural tendency to move diagonally across the body in the direction the shoulders are pointing . . . parallel to the net.

Errors are usually fewer from volleying forehands with an open stance (feet and shoulders facing the net), because you don't have to be as accurate when you volley. You have the whole court to aim for at the net and a wider margin for error. That's why people don't miss as often with an open stance forehand volley as they do with forehand groundstrokes, therefore are not as motivated to adjust the flaw, let alone notice it. That is also why this 'Braced' stroke, of the four covered here, will be the most underestimated . . . and ignored. I had the same hesitation when transforming my game. I thought my forehand volley was good enough. I still don't use it as often as I should. But when I do, it feels so much different, and by different I mean better.

Wouldn't you want to hit that volley deep and accurate rather than take your chances and hope it falls somewhere in the court?

The first part of the volley is the backswing, although not really a wind up or swing back per se, like the somewhat looping groundstroke. It requires only a shoulder turn and raising of the hand and racquet to shoulder height or above. (**See Photograph K**) On low volleys, you lower your upper body, not just the racquet.

The Brace improves the backswing automatically. By pushing the right arm up and behind the body, the Brace not only causes an immediate backswing, but also brings the left shoulder with it, resulting in a proper upper body rotation. Then the Brace stops the backswing even with or slightly behind the right shoulder, preventing a long wind up and a late hit. In the backswing, both arms are bent, the elbows are close to the body and the wrist is cocked, but not locked. The forehand volley wrist can be relaxed and yet remain firm, unlike the backhand volley wrist, which weakens if it is bent too far back, away from the net.

The forehand volley can be done with some wrist movement for slow balls above net level. I won't recommend topspin volleys, but they are a fact of life. If you do it well, go ahead. What was true for groundstrokes is more so for volleys. If the feet cannot be turned sideways in time, which often happens, the upper body is capable of executing the proper volley.

The second part of the volley is the contact point or zone. (**See Photograph L**)

The Brace starts pulling the racquet arm down and through the ball early to meet the ball in front of the body, between you and the net. The shoulders do not rotate much during the volley because the volley is such a compact shot that there is only time for the arms to move into the ball. Mostly hand and arm action also causes a straighter volley and increases control. Try keeping your balance, and ideally, your weight leaning forward. It reinforces your stroke.

The Brace stretches the racquet hand forward quickly, helping you to meet the ball where you can see it. Since the ball is best hit in front of your body, the contact point is much shorter than for a groundstroke. The Brace keeps the stroke as straight as possible up to contact, since there is little that can be done after hitting the volley to change its direction.

The Brace also steadies and reinforces the racquet hand at contact, allowing solid control over the ball and a continuous forward movement through the ball, no matter how hard it is hit at you. The steady movement forward also conquers the tendency to chop down too severely at the volley. Your body and racquet form a moving wall that collide with the ball.

The follow through, the longest section of a volley, ends the volley just as a good volley ends the point. **(See Photograph M)**

The Brace helps aim the ball by guiding the racquet hand toward the target. The racquet moves gradually down and toward the net, then up and back to the ready position above the net, where you can await the next volley. Unlike the backhand, the forehand Brace does not release the right forearm throughout the volley because it can comfortably reach and guide all phases of the stroke. The follow through is kept low by the Brace, which prevents the ball from being hit up and long. When an overhead is called for, use the Brace initially to turn your shoulders, then release your forearm and hit it like a serve.

I recommend volleying with one grip for both sides. A modified Eastern backhand grip, with the palm on the top bevel of the handle, gives a beneficial natural slice to all volleys. Finally, the formula for the forehand volley is: **Push up/pull down.**

Photograph K . . . Forehand Volley Backswing

Photograph L . . . Forehand Volley Contact Point

Photograph M . . . Forehand Volley Follow Through

Chapter Five

Serve and Overhead

I'm not going to dwell long on these two strokes, along with other specialty shots, like lobs, half volleys, approach and drop shots. Some of them may or may not be affected and improved by the Brace. That's up to each individual. The serve and overhead may or may not be, depending on your own decision to adapt it to them. Let me explain. The backhand overhead is merely a high volley, so the Brace can add power and control to that stroke.

However, the forehand overhead is different. The key is footwork, then shoulder rotation, then a well-timed wrist snap. If the Brace helps you get your shoulders rotated quickly, by all means use it in the initial motion while turning. If you want to practice forehand overheads with your left hand resting on your right shoulder as a 'muscle memory' training technique, I think you'll be pleased with the resulting extra shoulder action. I don't use the Brace on overheads, but that doesn't mean someone out there won't develop a technique with it. Go for it . . . surpass your teacher. He doesn't mind.

The keys to the serve are similar to the overhead. Even footwork is a component. You need to stand in the correct position because the placement of your feet affects your serve. Start sideways to ensure plenty of shoulder rotation, with your feet comfortably apart to give good balance. Close your stance (left foot closer to right sideline than right foot) if you are comfortable with that angle. It will wind up your hips and shoulders more than normal. Every bit of extra torque can only help. Toss the ball up above your front toe and slightly higher than you can reach with your racquet. This high toss does three things. First, it forces you to get off your heels. Second, it gives you time to swing. Third, it gives you good angles into the court from that height.

All serves are different. The key is good timing and a smooth racquet acceleration generated by your hips, shoulders, elbow and wrist, in that order. Find a style that works, is consistent, and not harmful to your joints. As far as strategy goes, I recommend the Triple 75 rule. Statistically and strategically, based solely on the fact that you have the advantage of serving, you are favored to win the point on your first serve 75 percent of the time, anyway. That's the first 75. So why not get your first serve in more often? Hit it three quarter speed, 75%. Go for corners, not aces. You will accomplish at least two things. First, you'll play the points more confidently and aggressively. Second, you won't have to serve as many second serves, which will benefit you physically and psychologically. Thirdly, you can place them better at reduced speed. Placement before power, I always say. That's the second 75. The third 75 is related to the previous benefit. Your modified first serve will usually go in 75 percent of the time, leaving fewer times when you are forced to serve a second time and more likely, lose the point. It's a win/win situation. Try it.

Practice your second serve a thousand times. Before a match, hit mostly second serves. It reduces nerves when you are confident about it. Get so confident that you can hit one with your eyes closed. I've tried it. It's a good feeling to know that it's the most reliable shot in your repertoire. It consists of a lower toss, directly over your head, sometimes farther back, if your back is more flexible, and a different wrist snap. Think up, not out. A heavy spin is sometimes more effective than power. The better your second serve gets, the more confident and daring you will become with your first.

If you want a 'Brace' drill to improve your serve with, try this during practice. After you toss the ball in the air, reach back with your left hand and tap your right shoulder. Then proceed with your serve. The uncomfortable motion will remind you to twist, or coil, your shoulders prior to opening up your upper body and transferring all that torque into the ball. Many people use more arm than shoulder action when serving. Some turn and face the net right before tossing the ball. Ironically, this can cause undue stress on the rotator cuff, because the shoulders are not really being involved in the swing. If the shoulders are already open when the ball is tossed, that energy and torque are not available. If you are tossing the ball to your left, that's a good sign that your left shoulder has already rotated too much to be helpful during the serve. Find a way to get it back into the wind up, under your chin, before you hit the ball. Your serve will always be like your putting game in golf . . . it can collapse without warning. I know. I don't play much golf anymore. Keep the serve simple, consistent, and efficient.

Chapter Six

The Name and its Benefits

B . . . ackswing
R . . . each
A . . . cceleration
C . . . ontrol
E . . . lbow

B is for backswing, technically the second step in the swing. The first step is deciding whether to hit a forehand or a backhand, depending on which side the ball is approaching. The backswing is often late, causing the stroke to be hurried and shortened. Because of the location of the hitting arm, the backhand and forehand have different, if not opposite, backswings. On the backhand side, the arm drapes diagonally across the body and is for this reason shorter, since the shoulder of the right arm is now closer to the net. This makes the backswing of the backhand the most important phase of the swing. Why? Because it is the most physically uncomfortable and difficult action for the body to perform during the swing, it is often incomplete or improper. Also, the backhand side is physically weaker and building up racquet momentum is more difficult. There are not as many large muscle groups involved, compared to the forehand. A fully extended backswing is needed for racquet speed, ball control and power. The legs and shoulders have to contribute. No wonder most players gravitate toward using two hands, forfeiting the advantages that one hand offers.

Many players use their left hand to pull on the racquet throat to help rotate the upper body and bring that arm around to the correct backswing position. Often the body resists and the backswing is still not complete or early enough. Pulling on the racquet is not the solution because the racquet is not the problem, the shoulder is. Besides, racquet pulling can only assist the backswing.

The Brace backhand pulls back on the right forearm, thereby forcing the arm and shoulders to rotate fully and immediately. Soon this technique becomes comfortable and the arms work together. You can also use the Brace to sense the backswing height and adjust it for whatever stroke is needed. The forehand backswing is physically more direct (the hitting shoulder is behind the body), but complicated by the variety of methods there are to choose from. Stand three feet in front of a fence, facing the net and assume a backhand backswing. Your racquet won't touch the fence. Turn the other direction for a forehand backswing and the racquet reaches the fence. The forehand backswing cuts time and gains distance over the backhand. It's pure physics. The key to a good forehand backswing though is not racquet height or loop style, but shoulder rotation. Most mistakes are made on the forehand when players 'arm' the ball instead of 'hip/shouldering' it. That occurs when only the arm is brought back for the backswing and the shoulders and hips don't rotate enough. You know you are using your arm too much when it remains up and away from the body during the backswing, rather than moving down and in before contact. It may be easier to arm your forehands, but in the long run of a match, you'll find it quite tiring. The trunk and shoulders can last longer with less fatigue. Use them.

Think of the forehand as a whip. The cord is the arm and wrist. The handle is the torso. The cord would be quite ineffective without the movement of the handle. The Brace lengthens and strengthens the handle by connecting the left shoulder to the right arm. Even when the shoulders are rotating properly, too often their energy is wasted. This happens if the arm precedes the shoulders into the contact zone. This also happens when the shoulders open up too early. They expend their energy, then the arm follows afterward with a shot that lacks power and control.

The Brace improves the forehand backswing by pushing on the right arm while pulling the left shoulder sideways. This is vital to hit through

41

the ball with the shoulders instead of just slapping the ball with the arm. The Brace also senses and adjusts the racquet height to match the height of the ball.

The Brace performs opposite functions on each backswing phase. It pulls the backhand backswing and pushes the forehand backswing. But it does not operate independently. The Brace hand is connected to the left shoulder. When the shoulder rotates, the Brace responds, instantly transferring that action to the racquet arm. It cuts backswing time in half, improving your timing.

Before your arms start working together, you might feel the Brace and your left shoulder being pulled back while you bring your racquet back for a forehand. This perceived resistance disappears eventually. When your arms start working together as a single unit, neither arm dominates the other.

When the backswing on either side is complete, your shoulders have rotated, you are resting your chin on your front shoulder, and you are peering over that shoulder toward the ball.

R is for reach. Power is the obvious firstborn benefit of the Brace. Reach is his underappreciated brother. The Brace provides the power of two hands and the reach of one for both backhand and forehand strokes. Most start out skeptical about the latter.

The two-handed backhand sacrifices reach for other advantages, thereby requiring extra steps to get closer to the ball. Volleying is difficult, if not impossible, with two hands because the ball must be met so far in front of the body. For a backhand volley, the Brace allows for pushing the right forearm forward and then letting go without interfering with either wrist or racquet. Even while running or off balance, the Brace extends the reach by reinforcing the arm whether hitting late or away from the body. Even for balls close to the body, and off balance, reach is improved in the sense of more strength to hit through the ball with a reinforced racquet arm. The Brace gives the same reach as one hand because it is not holding onto the racquet grip.

Volleys on both sides are better because the Brace stretches the stroke forward, in front of the body and keeps it solid even at a distance. It's difficult to keep a short, sometimes awkward, stroke from stalling at contact, and ending up being only a block. A reinforced forearm controls the ball, whether low or high or way out in front.

The key to the backhand is the backswing. But the secret to a good forehand is the follow through. The follow through is the most difficult and uncomfortable phase of the forehand for the same reason the backswing is the weakness of the backhand. Before the backswing starts, the shoulders are pointing parallel to the net, and lazily want to stay there. The shoulders must rotate clockwise until they are perpendicular to the net and then return to parallel to allow a full follow through. Otherwise the arm just slaps the ball.

On the forehand finish, the Brace pulls on the right arm and shoulder, freeing it to follow through all the way around and up. The extra reach is a new muscle memory that is seldom done consciously, or comfortably, by most players. It extends the contact zone and improves control of the ball. It also lengthens the follow through, making placement easier.

A is for acceleration. Obviously, the two-handed backhand became popular because the racquet could be swung much faster than with one hand. The Brace provides even more racquet speed without the disadvantages of the two-hander.

The Brace can hold the racquet back until the last possible second for amazing deception. The stroke becomes faster, therefore the ball is seldom hit late.

Never hit a backhand late. Memorize that rule and you will eliminate most backhand errors. The Brace makes that resolution possible.

The forehand windup is often exaggerated to build up racquet speed. The Brace will allow you to minimize the windup, streamlining it and making it more efficient. Even if the racquet comes to a complete stop behind the body and below the ball, it doesn't matter because the pulling power of the Brace and the shoulders provides instant acceleration for the racquet. It's the speed at contact and beyond that matters. If your racquet can go from zero to 60 in a split second, you don't need a fancy windup that might all be window dressing anyway. If you miscalculate, it looks foolish. The Brace eliminates the need to build up momentum. Racquet acceleration is needed not only at the beginning of the swing, but just as importantly, when making contact with the ball. You may not notice it, but the ball always slows the racquet at contact. It's inevitable. And that's when things can go wrong.

Solid is the word for the feel the Brace gives to groundstrokes and volleys because it practically eliminates racquet stall at contact. The ball's impact is overpowered by the accelerating racquet during the contact zone and fewer errors result.

Volleys are more aggressive because the Brace provides instant acceleration forward. Fewer late blocks behind the body result since the Brace has the racquet moving forward when the one handed volley is just finishing the backswing.

Finally, acceleration also applies to the speed that the Brace can generate by pushing or pulling the racquet back for the backswing. You'll find that the Brace can move the racquet back before the oncoming ball even crosses the net. Your service returns will improve with an accelerated backswing, a sudden stop, and a quick forward stroke.

C is for control. You need control more than you need power. All things being equal, I believe consistency usually defeats power. The Brace bestows both. Control means getting the ball to go where, or do what, you want it to. If you aim or want to aim down the line and your swing does not follow that direction, you will not have control of the ball. If you want topspin and your swing does not impart the correct action, you will lose control. If you want depth and your follow through stops short, you lose control, and rallies.

Your mind can only do so much to control the ball. Your body must follow your wishes. But your body must have the tools to carry out the instructions given. The Brace gives total control over the body. It's mind over matter and racquet over ball. Your racquet control increases because the Brace provides more feel for and awareness of your hitting arm and control over its position. The most solid and steady contact zone possible occurs because the Brace guides the hitting arm not only through the ball but also toward the desired target and with the intended spin.

Generally, power comes first for people learning the Brace technique. Control follows when the wrist gets stronger and the arms begin working together smoothly and muscle memory is ingrained. Learn to relax and not rush progress. Be patient and accepting. Let the Brace work its magic on you. When you try and force things to work, it often has the opposite effect. A physically weaker person who is loose and smooth can usually hit harder than a stronger player who is tense and trying to hit too hard. I can't count the number of people with already flawed strokes who have tried this new technique, expecting instant results, and rejected it prematurely. If you give it time, you will reap the great reward of amazing consistency.

E is for elbow. This weak link in the backhand stroke is easily injured. Poor form and even constant use can damage this fragile joint.

The Brace not only straightens the arm for correct form, but also acts as a solid shock absorber between the racquet and the elbow. The shoulder is also spared from overwork. Not only can the Brace prevent elbow pain, but it may also relieve those who suffer from it already, simply by correcting hitting errors that were responsible. All this because their elbows will no longer be severely bent, leading the stroke, or absorbing damaging vibrations.

Those who formerly used two hands will keep the benefits they have acquired from that style while adding the advantages of one hand, which they reluctantly forfeited.

The forehand is also improved because the Brace holds the elbow close to the body. The elbow has a natural tendency to move up or out from the body because the rotating shoulders are much stronger than the arm. When they rotate, the elbow is often forced to bend so the arm can control the swing. The Brace holds the elbow in so all the shoulder strength is transferred into the ball.

While volleying, the Brace actually trains the elbow to remain relatively still by exerting influence upon the forearm to help it and the wrist do most of the work.

Chapter Seven

Focus

Visual (Sight)
Auditory (Hearing)
Kinesthetic (Touch/Feeling)

Educators tell us these are the three different ways people learn. You learn by (1)seeing something demonstrated and/or performed, (2) hearing it recited and/or explained, or (3)by touching it and/or doing it. Everyone is different and no single teaching method is the best. For some, only one method works for them. For others, a combination of the three is most effective. Teachers have the challenge of discovering which effective formula works for each student. I admire school teachers. Their curriculum is far more difficult to share than this simple sport.

We are told to explore all learning styles and take advantage of the most effective method for us individually. So, any method I advocate is subjective. You must adapt whatever method I discuss here to your situation. It will work for you if you are predisposed to that technique, or you persevere and force it to work. Learning is a very subjective experience. So take the following information and interpret it to fit your situation. No two minds are identical and no two players are the same.

What works for me, may or may not work for you. Something here can be helpful, because the goal is the same for everyone . . . to master the subject.

Concentration is hard, you say? Of course it is, if you feel it is something you must try hard to do. One may also feel that squinting will improve your vision. It will for a while, but it is terribly exhausting and it looks silly. There is an easier way to improve your ability to concentrate.

All you need to do is be able to count to two. You see, what are we 'trying' to concentrate on? The ball, right? Well, then, if we are always watching the ball, how come we cannot concentrate on it?

You may be observing the ball itself, but you might not be as aware of its motion, speed or direction, and subsequently, of the necessary actions that you should be performing in response to it, as you could be. In other words, you might be in 'lazy mental automatic pilot.' That may be causing you to make some mistakes while hitting it, or failing to react as quickly as you could.

The flight of the ball can be broken down into three phases. The ball is either (1)coming toward you, (2)motionless, or (3)moving away from you. Test this situation during a game of catch with a partner. When the other person throws the ball to you, it is approaching, therefore it is in phase one of its path. The moment you catch it, it has become motionless. Basically, it is under your control and about to reverse direction. When you throw the ball back to your friend, it has entered phase three, traveling in the opposite direction. For your catch partner, you will notice this process of phases is reversed. Phase one for you, the approach of the ball, has become phase three from his perspective.

Does it take a lot of mental or physical work to play catch? Do you need to tell yourself to turn your body or move your feet over a little to the right or left and then lift your arm above your head and open your fingers to receive the object coming through the air? I hope not! And if you expressed all these instructions out loud every time you played catch and every time you caught the ball, well, your friends would not play catch with you again. Playing catch is fun. How many instructions do you need to give a little child when you first explain how the game goes? You just tell them to hold out their hands and you throw the ball into them. It's even fun when they miss. Do you ever tell them to try harder? Or do you just let experience teach? Missing teaches, fun teaches, the whole process of catching teaches itself.

"Watch the ball" is about the only verbal advice one needs to remind a child once in a while at the beginning. Soon, concentration is natural and easy, not something you must 'try to do,' or force your mind to work on.

Enjoyment of the game brings relaxation, and relaxation, or the absence of stress, brings focused concentration, or rapt attention, which has a more positive sense to it.

I'm sure you can picture a typical coach yelling to his worried athlete who has just made an error, "Concentrate harder!" This often backfires with more errors. Maybe the same coach might have been more effective with a friendly, "Just have fun," and the performance that followed would have amazed him.

There have been times when a person was so involved with the enjoyment of observing his body participate in a game that he or she has performed a remarkable shot and said afterwards, "I couldn't do that again if I **tried**!" It's probably true and it also demonstrates the illusion we are under that 'trying' is the way to concentration and peak performance.

Tennis is like catch. Even if it is more complicated than catch, still it should be approached in the same way as a child starting to play catch. Timing and rhythm are the keys to hitting a tennis ball, just as they are to a good game of catch. Stay relaxed and loose to perform those fluid arm and body movements. Yet, you can't force yourself to stay loose. You can remind yourself to relax, but even this can be interpreted by your body as coercion, like our screaming coach, and backfire. This would bring the opposite result, a stressful, feigned, forced concentration mimicry. How can you lose (loose) yourself in the act of hitting the ball? Could the game of catch be the key to timing and rhythm?

Could the three phases of the ball's flight be the ticket to true concentration, or rapt attention? Let me explain how I came up with this novel conclusion. I used to have a mental list of instructions for my mind to repeat each time I hit the ball. You may think that is strange, but I once knew a guy on my varsity high school team, whose father taped little phrases typed out on tiny white labels along the shaft and handle of his racquet, for him to refer to once in a while. Like a tiny coach in his ear and literally on his throat. More like a monkey on his back. Did they make a difference? No, but I actually thought about copying him. My method was simply a mental list of what I perceived as the fundamentals, refined down to the bare minimum and in the form of a slogan that was brief, catchy, and easy to remember and follow. The phrase was helpful, at best. Yet it was obviously impossible to repeat it to myself every time I swung at the ball, although I tried. So, I would occasionally remind myself of these buzzwords whenever I thought I was not focusing enough. But how did I decide or notice when I was not focusing? Is there a half-focused state? Whenever I lost a point, was it because I didn't focus? Couldn't it have been just a great shot by my opponent to end a point during which I had in fact played well? Several times I would remind myself of the special phrase and lose the very next point anyway.

Sometimes I would not repeat it to myself and play well. Where was my mind on those special occasions? I was intrigued by the dynamics of concentration and how it related to performance. Slogans were obviously not the way to pure, dare I say Zen-like, concentration. These instructions, however brief and simplified, were still verbal (and wordy) instructions stealing my attention and fragmenting the whole process of hitting the ball. While useful, external instructions were somewhat distracting.

Basically, the physical body already knows the fundamentals intimately, having learned them by trial end error, like the game of catch. The body is a kinesthetic machine. It learns by doing. It has no ears and eyes, only touch and feel. So words are meaningless to it. The body has been lectured to by you or an instructor while learning the game. If anything, the body would like help with the more complicated details. The guy with the notes pasted all over his racquet only succeeded in making his racquet heavier. That did not help the body play better.

I tried different concentration techniques and ideas. They made me realize that just letting my body do its job and being more aware of where the ball was and what my racquet was doing was far superior and more effective than verbal and mental input, however basic or catchy.

For example, once I noticed a teaching phrase, Feet-Firm-Follow. Phrases that all start with the same letter are a useful memory tool. This would remind the body to move its feet to the ball while getting sideways, keep the wrist firm at the contact point, then follow through toward the target to guide the ball. Everything seems covered, right?

There are hundreds of variations on this theme, depending on your version of fundamentals. Simplified concentration methods helped a great deal. They also helped me enjoy tennis more. But where was that perfect phrase that covered everything I needed? I knew the phrase should focus, no pun intended, on **mental** focusing and not mechanical swinging.

But then a strange and ironic thing happened to me over the weeks that I tried to convert from my former 'Fundamentals Formula' to a less instructive and intrusive attitude. I started trying to come up with new word lists to express verbally the importance of concentrating and relaxing, believing I had to remind myself of these basic principles. I had the right idea in transferring to a more low-key approach rather than worrying and harping on the externals, but now I was reverting to the same old habit of wanting something for my mind to keep nagging my body about just to maintain control over the body. The mind is a lot like a back seat driver who refuses to just shut up, admire the scenery, and enjoy the ride.

So, instead of being anxious about what my body was doing about moving, now I was being anxious about whether or not my body was staying relaxed. It was the same old broken record, but now it was playing a different song, over and over. I had managed to jump out of the fire, but I was still in the frying pan. Not quite as bad, but still room for improvement. My inborn tendency, as a writer, to want words to live and swing by, had prevented the full application of these pure concepts and principles that are wordless, beyond words; a state to be experienced, not described.

I now needed a nonacademic method to transmit the ideas of relaxed focus or rapt attention without nagging my body into performing it. Since the cardinal aim of focus was the ball and timing was the key to swinging correctly, I stumbled upon the numbers 1 and 2 to determine not only the way to watch the ball itself, but also the way to observe its position at any given point.

Since, in tennis, once the ball is thrown, it is out of your control, I have eliminated this as a phase to count. That leaves only two steps to focus on.

Phase One: From the opponent's racquet, crossing the net, bouncing (unless volleyed) and making contact with your racquet.

Phase Two: From your racquet, crossing the net, bouncing (unless volleyed) and making contact with your opponent's racquet.

Like playing catch, the path of the tennis ball follows two stages, or directions. Two players just play catch with their racquets, the difference being that you are returning, or throwing, the ball back and forth a little sooner and hoping or expecting your opponent to eventually miss.

Let's take this visual flow and transform it into a counting exercise. Since I want you to increase your focus on the ball once it crosses the net, let's narrow our concentration to the phase of the ball once it crosses the net. Obviously, when you see the ball hit by your opponent, your body reacts and your feet move you silently toward the side of the court the ball is heading.

The moment the ball actually bounces on the ground, silently say "**ONE (1)**" to yourself, or out loud while training, until it has become a habit.

At the exact moment your racquet makes contact with the ball, simply say, whisper or think "**TWO (2)**."

Add no instructions, just the number that corresponds to their respective ball phases, exactly at the moment it occurs. Be as precise as possible. The more precise you get, the more effective you will become at focusing on the ball and making solid contact with it. I guarantee. But be warned. It's not as easy as it sounds. You must pay attention to follow the ball's path and time its activity. 'That's the way the ball bounces,' isn't just a platitude. It's a challenge to monitor a unique and complicated motion. Remember when you were a beginner and the ball's movements seemed so overwhelming and unpredictable. Eventually it got more predictable and manageable. This new technique will bring that process to a new level.

Create your own version of this effective 1-2 mantra. Find your own rhythm. You can stretch out the sound of **1** (Whaaan, I keep it short, one, then silence/focus) to extend from the point of the bounce until your racquet strikes the ball (**2**). Some players time their exhale to match this brief contact phase, another feature to improve focus and timing. Other players time their backswings to coincide with the bounce of the ball. The location of the ball and its corresponding number reminds you, wordlessly and effortlessly, where your backswing and forward swing should be.

Your focus phrase will stretch or shorten depending on the pace of the ball. Like snowflakes, no two balls spin and bounce exactly the same way.

The ball will never become perfectly predictable. But the numbers 1 and 2 never change. Another advantage to counting out the path of the ball instead of merely observing it and reacting, is that it appears to slow down for you. By breaking the path of the ball into two distinct parts, your mind divides and stretches time, giving you the pleasant illusion of having more than you thought. Increased focus results in improved reflexes. The two go hand in hand and feed each other.

If you use this simple number system for your timing instead of instructions, your body and racquet will react instinctively to the ball to hit it properly and you will even find your racquet holding the ball on the strings a little longer as your increased awareness of phase 2, contact, stretches it out, almost like watching slow motion. The effect of this simple meditative technique, bordering on the hypnotic, on the body will be more relaxation and better performance. The ball will slow down while your body speeds up. That's what the 'Zone' feels like. And you'll find access to it more at will than by accident. When the mind assists with something helpful, like keeping time, the body is free to do what it was programmed to do, without receiving worthless instruction.

Counting to two is something that easily becomes automatic. And if you find your concentration slipping during a match, try whispering the numbers a few times to groove the habit deeper. It's a great way to get your mind back on the focus track. I'd love to see this become a universal technique, especially for beginners.

I brought my game to a better level with this simple technique. My confidence and timing improved dramatically, above and beyond what the Brace did for me. I was no longer over-analyzing every detail of every swing. Sure, my previous formula was basic, but all the details are connected to them, because they are words and ideas. When I faithfully use my 1-2 secret, I follow the ball like a hawk and my attention is focused like a laser. The ball slows down. You see it spin, then you watch the ball hit the strings every time. Your body and racquet movements become smooth and automatic, not deliberate and forced, as though dictated by inner orders. Just tell the body what the ball is doing, then trust it to handle everything. The 1-2 focus method helps instinct take over. You almost become an amused and amazed spectator of your own playing.

Verbal instructions are impossible, so don't use them. You'll have more fun too. The Brace method will give you the mechanics, the 1-2 focus method will provide the proper temperament. You will find yourself moving into the 'Zone' more often. You'll be relaxed, attentive and reaching your full potential because that nagging, critical voice inside is finally quiet. Previously, I gave you the slogan, "Keep your eye on the ball and the Brace will do it all." Now, you have the foolproof way to do just that. You have everything you need in these two forms of improvement.

For me, that wordy, subconscious echo that inevitably accompanied my previous instruction formula is gone. That echo of mind/body banter, that I had mistakenly assumed would be eliminated by a catchy instructional phrase, was now silenced by counting to two! What a simple solution.

You might ask, why say anything to yourself? Why not just use nothing? Because the mind needs a focus point, like a laser needs a target. The ball is the target. The location of the ball is the focus point. The real struggle is to let go of the imagined need for words, as if the trained body needs instruction, however simple they might be. The bored mind is trying to reassure itself that the body is doing it right, even though using words is no guarantee the body is going to obey them.

When you are focusing on the path of the ball (1 and 2), your body will react more quickly to it, because it is now freed to move without hindrance or hesitancy. The racquet will respond to the ball just as the hand automatically reaches for the ball during a game of catch. The racquet will move more smoothly, now that you are no longer concerned with the parts of the swing, only the location of the ball. Having done it many times, you know your swing will take care of itself.

Some may wonder if this 1-2 idea is just another form of instruction, only using numbers instead of words. Well, in a way it is the mind giving instruction to the body. But the difference is this instruction, or rather information, is something the body does not know already. The eyes do not technically belong to the 'body.' When I say, 'mind,' I mean the head and eyes, the brains of the operation as opposed to the brawn, the muscle.

For example, when your mind says to your body, "Bend your knees," your body protests and even snipes, "I know, I know. I've done it a thousand times!" Your body is right, it has done it a thousand times, correctly. It is instinctive. "Bend the knees" is a redundant and quite irritating command from the non-physical mind. It often results in just the opposite response from your body. Why? I'm not a shrink, so I won't analyze it. But when the mind, using the eyes which are vital to the 'blind' body, says to the body "One," which is easily translated to, "The ball just struck the ground," this is valuable, helpful, and nonjudgmental information to the body. The body can now begin preparing to hit it. This is vital information that the body, lacking eyes, cannot gain on its own. The mind can contribute vital information to the body that the body needs, and the body can be free to perform the only task it is assigned to, without undue interference from the mind. They make a perfect couple when the mind limits itself to its area of expertise, informing the body exactly where the ball is at all times: stage 1 (bounce) or stage 2 (contact). The mind thereby avoids repetitious physical instructions, the area in which it does not have practical experience. It sticks to what it does best, reminding the body when to swing, not how.

If your eyes are wandering away from their main duty to follow the ball, that's a pretty good sign that your mind is too. Why are our eyes and minds somewhere else? Why do we have such a tough time staying in the present? We spoil our enjoyment and miss our full potential.

Lets face it, our minds are often overactive. Admit it, your mind wanders all the time. Maybe right now. It's a long and technical chapter. When you're not thinking about actually hitting the ball correctly, you're thinking about the people on the next court, your car problems, your financial problems, etc. Why, because the mind is in nonstop hyper-drive. Thousands of thoughts race through it like moths around a floodlight. It's a supercomputer that never sleeps, even at night. Like a mantra during meditation, the 1-2 focus technique tends to push out the extraneous trivia that muddy the waters of your thoughts. Try it, you'll soon be forgetting about taking your car in for an oil change, or changing brokers, or doubles partners, and start seeing the ball like never before.

As in life, so with tennis. You may as well be present in this present moment, otherwise you'll miss out on the potential for enjoyment and accomplishment. In the words of an ancient sage, If not now, when? Trust me, all your problems will still be waiting for you when you get off the court. They're not going anywhere. So why not ignore them while you are striking the ball? I know, easier said than done. But made easily done with the 1-2 counting method.

Test yourself constantly, in life and on the court, whether you are truly focused on the task at hand, either hitting the ball or living each moment to the fullest. On the court, there are many methods to use. One I use once in a while is a simple, quick survey after hitting the ball, during rallying. I ask myself exactly how far from the service line the ball bounced and exactly how far from the baseline I struck the ball. A quick mental answer might be, two feet past the service line and three feet in front of the baseline. Or make a mental measurement of the space between where the ball bounced and where your racquet struck it. It is always different. A half volley is a few inches. A ball that bounces in the forecourt might travel several yards before it reaches you. Make a game out of it. Try and get identical answers, three feet past the service line and three feet inside the baseline. That's proof you were counting both phases and really saw it all the way. Or two shots in a row were exactly three feet from bounce to impact. Or make it more pressure filled, like a random drug test. Every once in a while, ask for the measurements to see if you are really paying attention to the ball. Vary the measurements. The first requested measurement was the gap between the bounce and impact, the next request was the distance from the service line and the baseline. These minor techniques will train you to be a ball hawk. It will become second nature, like living in the moment. The rewards are immense. Not watching the ball can become an insidious habit, always seeking to return. You'd be surprised how delinquent you can become without realizing it. With these techniques in place, like an alcoholic's sponsor, you never know when you are going to require from yourself an accounting, so you soon develop the habit of really seeing the ball, instead of lazily guessing where it might have been.

I can't improve upon Big Bill Tilden's advice. He devoted an entire chapter to watching the ball. He wisely counseled, "Never look at anything else." He was a man who practiced what he preached. He wouldn't have been great without following his own advice. He even acknowledged that there were some occasions when we were more susceptible to taking our eyes off the ball. I thought that was brilliant . . . Serves, Passing shots, Volleys, Overheads.

Finally, he gave four factors that make not focusing on the ball disastrous to good strokes.

1-The ball may be hit harder or softer than we first imagine, causing early or late hits.

2-The spin may be different than we predicted when we first saw the ball approach.

3-The ball isn't where we expected it to be. Wind, stupid!

I added that second word. I was talking to myself for all those shots I have missed because of the wind. No, I mean, because I took my eye off the ball on a windy day.

4-The court's surface may affect the ball after the bounce. We did not figure that into our prediction of where we thought the ball was going to end up.

Why didn't we just watch the ball all the way? Good question with a simple answer.

So much happens after the bounce, if you are even watching it then, which shows you must incorporate the entire 2-count phrase into your game, 1 (bounce) 2 (hit). Try it and you'll be hooked. But, if after all this persuasion, you still don't like using numbers, let me share with you a wise mantra given to me by a frustrated coach long time ago when I was having trouble concentrating on the fundamentals during either a match or practice, I don't remember which.

He said it all boils down to one simple phrase (He wasn't talking quietly at the time).

"SEE BALL-HIT BALL!" Thanks coach, I'll tape those words to my throat.

Now if you want to incorporate this phrase into your focusing efforts, even though I strongly recommend against verbalizing while stroking, you can substitute the word SEE for the number 1 when the ball bounces, and replace 2 with HIT when you hit the ball. Of course. "See" and "Hit" will accomplish a similar improvement in your timing and focus, but #'s work better.

See how that symbol jumps off the page better than a word? The action words are poor choices. You also 'see ball' when you hit the ball. Numbers do not convey distracting instruction. They are more helpful and less stressful.

My coach would be happy that he had helped so many thousands of new students with his irate ranting. It didn't help me at the time, but I have learned to apply his advice since. Below is the reason why words are less effective than counting. I'm only trying to steer you in the right direction, even though I can't force horses to drink once they reach the water.

An ironic example of role reversal is when your mind (or brain) tells your body "Watch the ball." The body replies (it has a mouth because in my book the mind and body share the mouth) "That's your job. All I do is hit the ball."

Whose job is it to watch the ball? The mind's job, the component that contains the eyes.

The only moveable part it controls, unless you can wiggle your ears. So if the mind is watching the ball, it should tell the body where it is, not how to hit it. The mind has one job, guiding the body to the ball. Don't think that this is automatic, training the mind to just count to two. It's easier said than done. It is a slow process. The mind is like a nosy director who wants to be the actor, editor, and screenwriter. He needs to be kept in his place. The mind of the tennis player must be demoted from being a similar control freak. It may be difficult to relieve it of all its former imagined duties and convince it to perform only one, even if it is the most important one. The results will convince the mind that it is better to do one thing perfectly than many things poorly. The active mind will eventually fall comfortably into its new role somewhere between disinterested spectator and meddling know-it-all. Peak performance is realized by the body when the mind is riveted on the ball, and cheers the body on rather than scolding its poor performance.

The mind soon starts helpfully coaching the body, "There it is, Go get it!" In other words, "You can do it." This perfect compromise is met by the mind that is relaxed, doesn't sweat the details of swinging, but is always alert to perform a specific function. Don't let your tennis experience get spoiled by anxiety over technique. (What am I doing wrong?) This analytical attitude can affect all levels of ability. Too much worrying about the technical side of 'hitting out' will overshadow the pure enjoyment of just plain out-and-out hitting. Concentration becomes effortless when you exert less effort to do it.

Two other things happen when you count during the ball's journey. The size and speed of the ball will appear to change. The mind increases its attention on the ball when it is drawn away from the surrounding distractions. The ball may not actually get bigger, but it might seem to. Not only size, but detail. Can you actually read the "Penn" label or the number on the ball, or detect its seams? You'll be delighted at what you notice when you stop trying to notice which way your opponent is leaning. There's only so much attention available. Delegate it to priorities.

The ball will also slow down, in your mind. If you monitor the path between the opponent's racquet and your side of the court, while you are awaiting the bounce, it ceases becoming an intimidating blur that you react to. Instead, you are already making decisions about its spin and your intentions. Then, after the bounce, the phase may shrink between 1 and 2, but the mind has already sped up and is not caught by surprise. Like an air traffic controller, the mind is relaying the ball's exact position and your body is instinctively preparing. Soon, you'll find yourself waiting with eager anticipation instead of fear and doubt. Slow motion is a common feeling among professional athletes who are engaged in perfect concentration. It's not reserved to a small elite group. It only takes training.

If you are someone who falls into the category of learning by seeing, the above information is for you. The majority fall into that category. However, this method can be tailored and altered for people who may respond better with hearing or listening. In such cases, you can adjust the phrase 1-2 to something that alerts you to the sound of the ball hitting the ground and then your racquet. You might want to keep using the numbers, but use them to coincide with the moments you hear the ball hit the ground, then your racquet. Most players tune out the sounds of the court. If you benefit from your auditory awareness of them, harness that ability. Personally, I feel deaf when I play.

For players who learn and respond to kinesthetic input, or touch and feel, become more aware of your body, especially your feet, and the racquet in your hand, since you cannot feel the moving ball. What are your feet doing when the ball bounces? What is your racquet doing when the ball bounces? Where is your weight shifting when you strike the ball? Put all these sensations into a short, helpful phrase, preferably with numbers. All of us should become more aware of all three sources of information during the swing. It can only help, as long as it aids our focus on the ball.

> Think "One" when the ball bounces
> When you hit it, whisper "Two"
> When it comes to helping out
> That's all the brain should do.

For raw beginners who need a foundation in the fundamentals before moving on to focusing and concentration, I do advocate two particularly helpful phrases that drive the basics of hitting into the memory. These phrases can even be spoken as each phase is put into practice, until they move on to counting. They differ slightly to account for the differences between forehand and backhand swings. First is the forehand phrase. Easy to remember, easier to execute.

Forehand: **Shoulders/Shoulders/Spin**

Let's face it. The forehand is just plain easier, to learn and perform. People have given up tennis because of their stinky backhands, but never because of a stinky forehand. Regardless, the forehand continues to cause as many unforced errors as the backhand during an average match. I don't have detailed statistics for this, it's just anecdotal input from several sources. So, it's vital that the forehand be learned to be a consistent stroke, not simply powerful.

The first word of this phrase is **Shoulders.**
It covers the initial step in preparation to hit the ball. You don't even have to move your feet to obey it. After turning the racquet in your hand to the forehand grip, twist the upper half of your body, at least your shoulders. Keep your feet wide apart and your knees bent. This will make it easier to rotate your upper body and hopefully your hips too. The more rigid your legs and knees, the more rigid your shoulders and hips will be. At least turn your shoulders so you are peering over your left shoulder at the ball. Your racquet goes back naturally when your shoulders turn.

The forehand backswing is easier because the arm holding the racquet is facing the back fence on the forehand swing. Don't worry too much about what the racquet is doing. Just try to feel it in your relaxed hand. 'When' you hit the ball is more important than 'How.' If you are using the Brace, learn to twist the racquet grip with one hand. It gets easier with practice. If you are like me and assume the ready position with your backhand grip (several advantages to this), you have eliminated this step on the backhand side.

The next word is also **Shoulders**.

It applies to the act of sending all that coiled power back into the ball. Your first shoulder turn started the racquet moving away from the ball at high speed. Now, like a whip, the racquet is accelerating back to the ball. If only the upper body twists because there isn't time to turn completely sideways with your feet, that's sufficient for a decent shot. Your feet and even your hips may or may not be involved, but your shoulders should always do most of the work. A shoulder dominated forehand is a strong and consistent one.

The third word in our simplified phrase is **Spin**.

I know what you're thinking. What, no mention of elbow position and follow through and wrist angle. I'll leave all that to Vic Braden. He's already covered it thoroughly. I just want you to feel your racquet brushing up the back of the ball. The shoulder/shoulder action will have given you all the momentum you need to finish the stroke with all your moving pieces in their correct places. If you want a drill for feeling the right spin, stand in front of a fence and brush your racquet up its face. That's what you want to do to the ball with your racquet. Your racquet acts like a windshield wiper. Keep your forehand formula simple and it will be simply great . . . **Shoulders/Shoulders/Spin**

Backhand: **Shoulders/Step/Speed**

This phrase is different than the forehand. The backhand is different from the forehand in several ways. With the forehand, the source of power and movement is the shoulders. With the backhand, it's the feet. Lazy shoulders ruin a forehand. Bad footwork sabotages the backhand.

The first word is **Shoulders**.

It is used only once in our formula because the shoulders are not as involved in the entire backhand swing as they are for the forehand. Upper body rotation is more important than actual footwork, especially on the forehand side. The main reason to rotate your shoulders at first is to get the racquet back as soon as possible and all the way. It is the first thing to do to get ready to swing. But poor footwork on the backhand side will impede shoulder rotation. All things being equal, the backhand side needs a more closed stance than the forehand, because of where the hitting shoulder is located. It has farther to travel to get to the backswing position. It needs more help from the feet to get the body turned sideways. The forehand side has all the advantages when it comes to getting the racquet back. The only thing that evens the playing field is footwork. The backhand backswing loses two feet in the process just from having the hitting shoulder move closer to the net during preparation, hence the need to stretch it to the maximum extension by getting the feet in a straight line to the net, or even closed.

The next word in the backhand phrase is **Step**.

Getting your right foot in front of your left does more than finish your backswing. It turns your body farther than a mere shoulder rotation could. So the word 'Turn' is relative and sometimes inadequate. If your shoulders and feet don't get out of the way of your racquet, you cannot swing fully and freely. That is why they must rotate and move. They both set up the final sequence of the swing. They allow the greatest distance away from the ball, just like a taxiing plane must start at the far end of a runway. It needs momentum to take off.

The third word is **Speed**.

I don't use this word for the forehand because it comes naturally on that side. It does not need special attention. Racquet speed is the bane of the backhand. It's why most beginners switch to two hands. Out of desperation to swing faster. If you don't neglect the first two phases of

this phrase, you will succeed at the last. The longer the backswing, the more racquet speed you can generate and the better you can place the ball. Facing the net on a backhand makes it difficult to hit hard and accurately. Topspin is stressed in phase three of the forehand formula, but not so much on the backhand. The wrist is usually dormant. The feet and arms usually create the spin needed for control and consistency. The final word covers the actual swing, which leaves out all the technical aspects of it and simply reminds you that it is not so important how you hit the ball as when. See the next chapter to learn more about timing. With the Brace, you are free to add as much wrist action as you feel comfortable with.
Shoulders/Step/Speed

Chapter Eight

See-Speed-Swing Strategy

There are not many fundamentals in tennis. Otherwise, they wouldn't be called fundamentals. If the list became too long, it would defeat the purpose of having them. Let's face it, it's not brain surgery. Those who take the fundamentals for granted, who instead like to concentrate on the more complicated aspects of stroking and strategy, can't see the forest for the trees, in my opinion.

Why bother keeping your wrist cocked at a 26 degree angle when you don't keep your eye on the ball? Now, I know that some readers with a tendency to 'get technical' are going to say to themselves, "Is it really supposed to be 26 degrees?" That was just a test to see how hooked on the fine points some of us are, splitting hairs while the truly important things are neglected. I don't even know how many degrees it is. Ask Vic Braden. He'd know. There might be more fundamentals to stroke technique than we realize. It may be a subjective thing that varies from teacher to teacher. Here's my opinion on strategy, not mechanics.

The basics of tennis strategy are three. These three fundamentals have as their single goal . . . consistency. No strategy, however fancy and technical, is worth anything without consistency. The player who could get every single ball back would never lose. Few such players exist. Consistency as a purely defensive strategy cannot work. But consistent play coupled with offensive strategy is an unbeatable combination.

The strategy slogan that I have chosen and utilize is See-Speed-Swing. It may seem harmless enough, it may not even sound much like an effective strategy. It may even sound more like mechanics than strategy.

But once we analyze it thoroughly, you may want to adopt it for your strategy slogan. It is important to stress at this time that this is not a slogan that replaces the 1-2 timing/focus method I advocate and use (think or whisper) while actually hitting the ball. This **3-S strategy** is only a guide or checklist to use during rests and changeovers to analyze myself to see if I have been applying the fundamentals during play. If not, then nothing else is going to work. This 3-S strategy will quickly reveal the flaw in your game plan that may be causing you problems. Let's examine it in detail.

SEE:

Watch the ball. How many times have you heard that order? More importantly, how many times have you not done it when you hit the ball? I would venture to say that most of us neglect this basic rule more than half the time. Do you even know whether or not you are watching the ball? You may think this simple rule is redundant, but almost every miss is in some way related to the failure to follow the ball as well as you could have. In fact, it is almost impossible to miss the ball when you are watching it. If you are wondering what watching the ball has to do with strategy . . . Everything!

What is one of the main causes of unforced errors, but failure to watch the ball as closely as you could have, which is also a dead giveaway that you lost concentration momentarily. What is the best strategy in the world? Bjorn Borg will tell you that just getting everything back helped him win 5 Wimbledon Championships in row. They were played on grass, no less.

"All right," you say, "if I watch the ball I will not miss very often. But I need to hit hard and aim for the corners to win points. How can watching the ball really help me do that?"

First things first. You cannot aim the ball until you make contact with the ball. It does no good to follow through toward your target until you have made solid contact with the ball that is bound for that target. It doesn't matter how hard you swing if you miss-hit the ball while swinging. Everything hinges on the contact point or zone. Using the 1-2 focus method is going to help you watch the ball all the way to the racquet because you must know when you make contact with the ball to know the precise moment that the path of the ball changes from point 1 to point 2. Watching the ball may never become a habit. The eyes get lazy and bored. They wander for no reason than to track surrounding movement. It takes discipline and 1-2 focusing to keep them on the job. It takes constant vigilance to keep the eyes involved where they belong. If you have to, count to 2 with each ball on every point.

Some people say watching the ball all the way to the racquet is physically impossible, because all the eye sees is a blur. No, that is only true of the path of the ball as it leaves the racquet at full speed. The approaching ball is never moving faster than they eye can clearly see. The blink reflex may cause us to not want to look at the ball meeting the racquet, but whenever we overcome the habit of looking elsewhere and start to focus on that impact point, it is not blurry, until after contact. We even have the tendency to look away when we are serving. The ball is certainly not blurred then, is it? Sometimes there is a physical cause. The opening shoulders tend to pull the head and neck away from the stroke. But the reason is usually psychological. You may feel that hitting the ball is such child's play that you have outgrown the need for this petty fundamental. "Watching the ball is for beginners, not me. I can do it with my eyes closed."

Yes, I suppose you can. Most of the time you do. But is that contact always solid, always in front, always confident? It cannot be. You just cannot be consistent with your eyes closed, or at best, somewhere else.

Seeing the ball is easier on the volley, because the volley is instinctively hit out in front of the body, closer to the net and in better visual range. Serves and overheads are also easier to keep watch of because you have to. The ball will hit you on the head if you take your eye off it. We are also more alert during these strokes because the speed and position of the ball causes our reflexes to sharpen instinctively. The pressure seems greater in relation to the difficulty of the shot and our senses sharpen accordingly.

Groundstrokes are a different story. Yet, groundstrokes seem easier. The opposite is true. The ball is actually more difficult to hit because it is not only spinning more off the ground, but also changing direction faster. Then why do we relax and guess at the position of the ball and swing where we think it might be? There are many reasons. Our eyes get bored if we look at the same spot over and over. Our eyes are attracted to the movement across the net and even off the court. The ball actually travels too slow to challenge and stimulate the eyes. It's hard work, like listening to a boring speaker. The mind works ten times faster than the spoken word. It is no challenge. What can you do to keep the eyes interested in what is happening when the racquet and ball meet? It takes discipline. Let the eyes watch both the ball and the opponent while the ball is still at a safe distance. As the ball gets past the service line, the eyes must focus on it exclusively.

You can't do anything about your opponent's actions at this moment anyway and hopefully you have already decided what to do with the ball, so zero in on it. You have to watch it all the way to the racquet to know the exact moment in changes from point 1 to point 2. Get into the habit of using the 1-2 focus method and watching the ball will become instinctive. They go together and create a cycle that builds more concentration. Watching the ball makes it easier to count 1 and 2 at the correct moments they occur, and counting to 2 at those events makes it less boring to watch the ball and nothing else. You'll be encouraged by your newfound success when you achieve a new level of pure consistency. Winning is never boring.

The forehand stroke is more difficult to focus on than either the backhand or the volley. Not only is the ball contacted later, but the body is turning and forcing the head to turn, much like the service motion. Watching the ball can feel awkward, even difficult. Extra effort and monitoring is vital to maintain eye contact with every forehand.

For all these reasons, I chose this simple fundamental first and foremost.

It's the first thing to go, but not the hardest thing to get back. It's as easy as One-Two.

SPEED:

The second word of my basic strategy slogan has to do with shot selection. How do you decide what type of shot to hit? And how do you decide where to aim the ball? Often there are several choices available.

That can actually be detrimental to good performance. What about percentages? The key to a good strategy is using the correct shot in each situation. But how do you decide between topspin and slice, or crosscourt and down the line?

The speed of the ball is the key. The speed of the ball as it approaches should help you decide what to do with it. And if you have trained yourself with the basic rules of shot selection, you can decide your strategy immediately, instinctively. By saving time in the decision process, you will increase your chances of executing it correctly.

Basically, the speed of the ball is either fast, medium, or slow. There may be different heights and spins, but those details are usually irrelevant. Your automatic strategy will usually cope with them.

If the ball comes at you at a fast speed, **always** hit it back crosscourt! Whether it comes at you crosscourt or down the line does not matter. Always hit it back crosscourt. Why? More points are lost by hitting shots wide than hitting them long. The reason why half of these points were lost was because the ball was hit late. The chances of hitting late increases with the speed of the ball. If you try to hit a ball down the line that is traveling fast, the probability that you will be late increases with the ball's velocity. It is a matter of percentages. The crosscourt shot has such a greater chance of going in, that your best strategy would be consistency, even if it were a defensive shot. Another factor involved shows why the percentages are so great in favor of a crosscourt shot. The down the line shot may seem just as easy, but what would happen if you hit the ball a fraction of a second late? The ball would go several feet wide and land out, right? But if you were aiming crosscourt and you made contact late, which is a stronger likelihood than hitting early, what would happen? The ball might still land several feet to the right of the intended target, but in this case that would be in the center of the court. You see, the margin for error is greater for a crosscourt shot when the ball is coming at you quickly, not to mention net height. By the term margin for error, I mean the odds of making a mistake. You want to put yourself in situations or make attempts that contain large margins for error. Late hits will still land in the court. Aiming down the line has a small margin for error, because a late hit will land wide. All those shots that would have gone in crosscourt are eliminated from your option list. If given a choice between a 75 percent chance of success and a 25 percent chance, the choice should be obvious. A prepared player has already decided ahead of time his first choice in several situations. That way, he can be better prepared for surprises. So, consistency would certainly help in shot selection, and instinctively going crosscourt in this situation will eliminate many unforced errors. And I guarantee, if you hit fewer unforced errors than your opponents, they will have a difficult time defeating you.

Though everyone knows to go crosscourt most of the time, not many know when to select the shot that goes down the sideline. The opposite rule applies for shot selection when the ball approaches slowly. The chances are greater now that you will hurry the stroke, therefore the ball should usually be hit down the line. The other half of the points lost from the ball going wide is because the ball was struck too early. If you attempt a down the line shot off a slow bouncing ball and you strike it early, which is common, the ball will still land safely inside the court. Notice how the margin for error has reversed itself with the change of the ball speed. It's simple physics. If your strategy is to use the highest percentage shot at all times, then the speed of the ball will dictate your selection, regardless of your opponent's position.

If you attempt a crosscourt shot on a slow ball, you may have more court to hit into than down the line, but the down the line shot may be the better option because of the timing factor. The chances of hitting wide on a crosscourt attempt actually increases with a slower ball speed. So, we see that the crosscourt shot is not always the highest percentage shot. Remember, the rule for ball speed is always crosscourt on a fast ball, and usually down the line for slow balls. This makes sure your shot selection is not too predictable to your opponent. Medium speeds fall somewhere in the middle of this range. Habits are not all that bad if the rate of success is increased.

The closer you are standing to the sideline, the greater your margin for error becomes for a crosscourt shot, because the amount of available court increases. Therefore, a slow ball that lands wide is the best possible situation for having both options, crosscourt or down the line. A slow ball that lands in the middle of the court is the worst possible time to elect to hit crosscourt, since the odds are great that you will hit early and the amount of court to aim for is at a minimum.

What about medium speed shots? This speed causes less timing trouble, so both choices are available. Exercise caution here that you do not meet the ball too early when choosing crosscourt or too late when choosing to hit down the line. Your number one goal is to get it in. Remember, an approaching topspin usually adds speed and sliced balls come at you slower.

What about your use of topspin or slice? How do you decide which to use? Do you just mix up your shots at random and throw in a slice once in a while to impress your opponent to show him you can hit a variety of shots? There should be a strategic reason behind your use of slice and topspin. The word speed also relates to how you should hit the ball, not just where. When the ball is fast and wide, like a hard serve to your backhand, or even to your forehand, the slice is the best percentage shot of all. Yes there is such a thing as a forehand slice, and although many players may spurn the stroke, it has kept me in countless points that I might otherwise have lost, and even won me some outright. The slice is not only consistent, but also stays low, offering the opponent little advantage or opportunity. It is slower, buying you time to recover from a poor court position.

Especially effective when your opponent hits a hard crosscourt approach shot, the forehand slice stays close to the top of the net and stays low, whether or not it bounces. More points have been thrown away by futile heroic attempts at sideline passing shots off fast groundstrokes because the ball was inevitably hit late, when a defensive slice would have kept the ball in play, at least until a better opportunity arose. I am always willing to hit several defensive strokes to an opponent at the net while waiting for the right moment, the high percentage passing shot, because the one at the net is under pressure to end the point.

When the ball approaches at a medium or slow speed the choices, for not only direction but also type of spin, increase. A topspin crosscourt is still the highest percentage shot. A slice down the line is more likely to go in than a topspin shot down the line. Why? Because the topspin stroke is just that, a stroke, a longer swing than the slice swing. Therefore, the chances of hitting late are higher for the topspin shot. So, the slower the ball, the safer either shot becomes when aimed down the line. Here is a guide chart to use for shot selection.

Ball Speed	Your Shot Selection	Success Percentage
Fast	Slice/Topspin crosscourt	High
Fast	Slice down the line	Medium
Fast	Topspin down the line	Low
Medium	Slice/Topspin crosscourt	High
Medium	Slice down the line	High
Medium	Topspin down the line	Medium
Slow	Slice down the line	High
Slow	Topspin down the line	High
Slow	Slice/Topspin crosscourt	Medium

This chart could be doubled. A separate one for the forehand and backhand. They would be only slightly different, so I won't be redundant. However, I probably return two thirds of my backhands crosscourt, simply because the down-the-line backhand is more difficult than the forehand. Hit down the line more often with your forehand (on medium speed shots) because it is easier to control the timing and there is naturally more confidence on that side. When returning serves, this chart is very helpful, because time is reduced and the swing must be shortened.

Where the ball approaches from is not as important as the speed of the ball, so either direction has basically the same percentage. Remember, according to the above chart, a crosscourt shot never earns a 'low' percentage rating. It should always be your first choice.

Suppose you receive a high-paced shot into your forehand corner. And suppose you have a slim chance of your risky down the line shot going in, even though it would be a sure winner, but a much greater chance of your crosscourt shot going in. I'd prefer an 80 percent chance on a predictable shot than a 20 percent chance on an outright winner. In fact, you'd be able to hit several of the safer versions to win a point. Otherwise, you might find yourself losing several points on high risk strokes for every one you successfully make.

This basic guide to shot selection also applies to volleying even more so than groundstrokes, because the margin for error is so much smaller.

A small margin for error means the odds of missing increase due to the higher level of difficulty. The ball speeds are greater and errors of only an inch or two in midair contact with the ball can translate into targets being missed by several feet. Therefore, safety and consistency are more important. You can get by with sloppiness and risk from the baseline, but rarely at the net. Being neither late nor early is the key to accurate volleying, even if it means becoming somewhat predictable.

Besides, almost all volleys that land in the court put pressure on the opponent. Volleys that go out bestow confidence to opponents.

Finally, the speed guide applies to the lob. The deep lob is worthless if it lands wide. To ensure that it never does, leaving you with only depth to worry about, always lob a fast paced ball crosscourt and use a defensive slice lob. Usually hit an offensive lob down the line off a slow paced ball, although you can mix these up in both directions. If your timing is off on either one it will probably still land in the court, hopefully near the baseline.

Obviously, you'd always want the ball to come back to you slowly, which has the highest overall success probability. But that isn't going to happen, unless you are playing someone unique. A mixture of speeds can be quite frustrating if you don't have a plan in place.

Program your mind to react instinctively to the speed of the ball. Otherwise you will waste valuable time deciding how and where to hit the ball. The more time you waste for shot selection, the less time remains for shot perfection. The reverse is also true.

The two most common errors in technique are what I call "The Two Eyes (I and I)."

1) An Incomplete swing:
2) Taking your eyes (**I**) off the ball.

Correct your **I**-sight and most other bad habits will vanish.

Use the Brace to cure the first "**I**" bad habit and my unique 1-2 Focus Method (discussed earlier) on the second "**I**" weakness and you've got the perfect combination. Other basics of a mental nature were also covered. I want to turn you into a perfect hitting machine, outside and inside.

For the sake of simplicity, let's say all balls hit at you arrive at three different speeds: Fast, Medium, and Slow. Let's say they average 5, 25, or 50 miles per hour. The 5-25-50 rule says that in order to eliminate half of your unforced errors (the other half are equally divided between those balls that go long and those that hit the net), use this strategy to eliminate ever hitting wide right or left, by lowing your margin for error and ensuring that your late and early hits still go in the court. Isn't that what you want? The one who gets the ball back one last time wins the point. So increase your odds of doing that with this strategy. You might object, "but my opponent will figure out my system." Not true. There is still enough leeway in the formula to allow an element of unpredictability. Even if he does anticipate correctly, he still has to return the shots. And there will be many more consistent ones to boot, while running corner to corner. Anticipation becomes irrelevant, compared to a two to one ratio of winners to unforced errors.

SWING:

This third key word may not seem to have anything to do with strategy, but as with direction, so stroke mechanics are the bedrock of consistency. And consistency is the key to success. What is more fundamental than the swing itself? What is more beneficial than a proper swing? Your swing was flawed if you missed your shot. How, though, do you pinpoint the flaw with so many phases to choose from and so many factors involved in swinging?

The key phrase which you should memorize by writing it down a thousand times is:

Backhand/backswing . . . Forehand/follow through

Nine times out of ten, maybe all ten times, something goes wrong with your swing, it is probably opposite phases of the two strokes, as listed above. Why would the backswing go wrong on the backhand stroke and the follow through on the forehand? Because the backhand follow through and the forehand backswing are relatively effortless, compared to their counterpart phases, and difficult to wreck.

This is because of shoulder position. It operates comfortably on the follow through side of the body during backhand and the backswing side during the forehand. This location makes these two phases of the swing relatively easy and effortless and, at the same time, makes their counterparts uncomfortable, cramped, awkward, and prone to error.

The crucial motion during both vulnerable phases is the rotation of the hitting shoulder from right to left, or counterclockwise for right handed players. This is also the most difficult and neglected phase. The arm must drape across the body and sometimes the lazy shoulders and poor footwork often complicate things, or just get in the way. This rotation takes place during the first phase of the backhand stroke and the third phase of the forehand stroke. If either of these vital phases is neglected, you are left with half a stroke. The backhand follow through rarely gives you a problem because the arm is simply uncoiling freely and catching up with the shoulder. The forehand backswing usually works fine, despite its infinite variety among players. As soon as you barely pivot sideways, your backswing is ready. The forehand is more complicated because it requires two shoulder rotations, whereas the backhand is basically one.

Therefore, when analyzing the swing, as part of a strategy, you only need to isolate which side is giving you trouble, and then observe whether that part of the swing is being done properly. First of all, the Brace teaches new muscle memory by pulling the backhand backswing, and the forehand follow through to its maximum extent. So, half the battle is making sure to use it all the time. Secondly, the footwork can influence these phases of the swing, either hindering or helping. A more open stance on the forehand can give you the best of both worlds. Your backswing will not be seriously affected by leaving your feet at a 45 degree angle, pointing toward the left net post. This will free your hips and shoulders to rotate more freely and not restrict your follow through. This will give you more room to continue swinging up and out, instead of around and across your body prematurely. The opposite situation for the backhand warrants the opposite advice. Close the stance to lengthen the backswing, with the lead (right) foot crossing over so that your back is partially visible to your opponent, like a left handed baseball pitcher during his windup. This gets the hips and shoulders out of the way, enabling you to take the racquet all the way back and down, rather than up and away from the body. Use the Brace to make it automatic, so even if there is not time to move your feet around to a closed stance, at least your shoulders will rotate, allowing a full backswing.

Here is another way the forehand differs from the backhand:

Forehand: Contact with the ball is made during the first half of the stroke. Speed is increased after impact. Power is provided by shoulders and hips, and added wrist.

Backhand: Contact is made during the second half of the stroke. Momentum is built up before impact. Power is provided by arms and legs lifting up, some from shoulders, little wrist.

Here is one place where the question, "What am I doing wrong?" might be helpful.

The second message derived from the word 'Swing' is related to where the shoulder is located. It precedes the swing on the backhand, but it mirrors the arm during most of the forehand. This calls for a different contact point for maximum power, control, timing and consistency. These desirable things are possible when you concentrate on always hitting the backhand early, off the lead hip or earlier, and always hitting the forehand relatively late (compared to the backhand), off the belly button or later.

Since the consistency zone on the forehand extends from the back hip to the belly button, concentrate on waiting for the ball longer than for a backhand groundstroke. The forehand swing curves around the body toward the follow through. If you meet the ball too early, too far in front of the body, the swing is not only rising sharply, but it is curving to the left. You're really making contact near the tail end of the ideal zone. You will be unable to safely hold the ball on the strings with that curving contact zone. You might be forced to make corrections that wouldn't have been necessary had you patiently waited a split second later. Most people have a real phobia about holding the ball for any length of time on the racquet. They want to make contact and release immediately, sacrificing control, spin, and depth. When you wait until the ball is farther back, not past the body, but even with your trunk, where your true power is, you will experience a longer contact zone, and more confidence. You will no longer be stretching forward and slapping at, lifting, or scooping the ball.

The opposite is true of the backhand stroke. The arm is a pendulum that travels in a relatively straight line and has no problem with a long contact zone. The need for momentum is why there is a need for an extra long backswing. It is also more difficult to get the racquet under the ball because there is less reach on the backhand backswing than the forehand. The arm must cross over the body diagonally. If the arm is bent, the backswing can get too high. The less distance that the racquet travels, the less speed it can achieve. Already, you've got two problems with a late hit, high backswing and slow racquet acceleration. The ball usually wins that contest.

Thus racquet speed is more crucial during the backhand than the forehand, since the backhand has less power during contact. I like a low backswing. Some advocate a high backswing in case you have to hit a slice backhand at the last minute. However, since the two shots have such a similar backswing, you can quickly lift your racquet when you decide on the slice. Besides, it is better to hit a flatter slice because your backswing was too low, than to hit a topspin into the net because your backswing was too high. The higher the backswing, the shorter it becomes. It is a game of inches and you can't afford to waste any.

More backswing on the backhand means less shoulder action during the swing, which is good. Too much shoulder rotation turns the follow through into a mimic baseball swing, which I feel should be reserved to the forehand. The contact zone curves to the right and cannot hold the ball safely on the strings. Less backswing on the forehand, however, is good. The racquet stays low and close to the body and when swung with the shoulders will carry up and away from the body, toward the net during contact. It's what your racquet does after contact that matters most. Let me illustrate the difference between the two strokes again at the risk of sounding repetitive. The backhand backswing is like reaching into your left pants pocket. The forehand backswing is simply the right pants pocket. Try the two. There is a big difference. One side is comfortable, the other is not. The backhand requires more stretching to get to the correct position. The follow through for each side is also opposite. The backhand follow through is simply raising your hand, like you would to wave to a friend. No problem. The forehand follow through is like trying to scratch your left ear with your right hand. Do you see the extra effort needed to both reach into your left pants pocket with your right hand, or scratch your left ear with your right hand. Both of these actions are uncomfortable, and yet we must perform one of them with each groundstroke. If these motions are flawed, so is our swing going to be. And without your awareness, these two motions may be suffering in your technique. If we concentrate more on performing the difficult phases of the swing, the other parts are going to take care of themselves automatically. Try it. Isolate and become aware of just that key phase of the swing, and see if the whole stroke becomes more effective.

So, if you decide to adopt this formula for self-examination, periodically throughout a match or practice session, run down the three word checklist to see if there are any glaring weaknesses in either one. Are you falling short in the See-Speed-Swing checkup? Nine times out of ten, you will be able to troubleshoot your problem and fix it.

So, let's combine this principle with our 1-2 Focus method:

1)When hitting a backhand, at the count of One (the bounce of the ball), mentally check on your backswing by feeling your racquet go all the way back, from shoulder turn, footwork and arm movement, then down for topspin, up for slice. Either way, a complete backswing will usually determine a successful swing and follow through, because these final two phases are a natural result of a correct backswing.

2)When hitting the forehand, the first part is easier and almost automatic, shoulder turn, racquet back, footwork (optional, if time allows). Then, the shoulders must rotate again to allow the arm to reach up and around for a full follow through. If the shoulders don't rotate, the arm will resist and shortchange you on your follow through. Finally, you need a fast, full, free-flowing, follow through for a fine forehand. Okay, I like alliterations. To achieve this phase, focus on step Number 2 (contact) even more than you would on the backhand side. Contact (2) is the key number on both sides, true, but more important on the forehand side. Trust me. Okay, don't trust me. I'll tell you why to focus more on #2 for a forehand. Because contact is made later than on the backhand side.

There is a "Blind spot" on the forehand side where the ball can easily disappear, especially if you crane your head and neck up before impact. Unlike the backhand side, where you usually make contact off your front foot, forehand contact is sometimes as far back as your belly button, or even farther back, as far back as the back foot. The backhand impact area resembles the volley, out in front where it can be seen and controlled. Focus on Number 2 and this will train you to hit through the ball with the proper follow through. It's the weak link that you strengthen by focusing.

Advanced Brace Theory

The Wrist Wrap Brace is the best transition for people who already use the two handed backhand. It is more similar to their style, although nothing prevents them from changing to the L-Bow Brace if they become proficient at both methods and it better suits their needs for certain shots. Both Braces work equally well for volleying. Sometimes, I use the Wrist-Wrap Brace for groundstrokes, then switch to the L-Bow Brace when I rush the net. I might use the L-Bow Brace to receive a hard first serve, then switch to the Wrist-Wrap for the second, simply because I intend to slice the first and topspin the second and I have more confidence in their respective strengths in those specific areas. Find the one that works best for you. You might find that one Brace hold works better for your backhand and the other one works better for your forehand. Don't worry. You will eventually become as smooth at switching back and forth as you are with the different racquet grips or spins.

Granted, there is more variety of shot selection with the L-Bow Brace. The reason is obvious after you start experimenting with both of them. With the Wrist-Wrap, there is only one comfortable place to hold on to your hitting arm, just above the wrist. Every other location, either higher or lower on the forearm seems awkward, to me at least. My only wiggle room when hitting with the Wrist-Wrap Brace is whether or not to let go after I hit a backhand groundstroke. I don't let go when I hit down the line. I do let go when I hit crosscourt, although follow through is only one factor in directing the ball. Otherwise, my Wrist-Wrap

Brace backhand is pretty much a clone (on steroids), very much like a conventional two-hander.

The opposite is true with the L-Bow Brace hold. For more or less leverage and power and control, you have the freedom of adjusting the position of your L-Bow grip on your forearm.

If you slide it down to your wrist, you will get a different feel and swing than if you move it up close to your elbow. If you find yourself hitting late against a power player, slide the Brace down nearer the wrist for a quicker, more compact swing. At the net, slide it down to the wrist for quicker hand movement and less wasted motion. For a bigger swing with more topspin and power, slide the L-Bow up to the elbow and you will see and feel the difference.

It's the same on the forehand side. For more shoulder action, slide the Brace up to the elbow. Or even to the bicep if you want to try the third type of Brace, recommended for people who feel too constricted with their free hand that low on their hitting forearm. No photograph provided. Your left (Brace) hand rests upon the bicep, above the elbow of the right arm. Allows more reach, with the same shoulder turn and racquet velocity.

Your biggest challenge is not technique, but timing. The Brace can accelerate the racquet so well that you might have too much of a good thing and find yourself hitting early. On the backhand, it's not that big a deal. It's better to be early on the backhand. But on the forehand side, too early is a problem. Too early wastes power. Learn to wait patiently. You will need less time for the actual swing so you have more time to prepare for and await the ball. Contact the ball between your hips, not too far out in front. Better late than early on the forehand side. I had more trouble perfecting the Brace on the forehand side, for that very reason. When timing and technique are combined, the Brace forehand is devastating.

You can actually adjust the L-Bow Brace to cope with different ball speeds and spins. If you move the Brace up or down your forearm, it will change the dynamics of your swing, leverage, racquet speed, etc. For instance, if the Brace is closer to your elbow when you hit the forehand, your shoulders will open earlier and your racquet arm will follow with more reach. Do this, for instance, when the ball bounces slow or low. Experiment and discover what it can do for you.

Remember to relax while you adapt the Brace to your style. Don't force it to work. When you tense up it prevents the involved body parts from working together harmoniously.

Finally, the main struggle you will have applying this method to your strokes is psychological. If trying the Brace seems strange, weird, uncomfortable, odd, or impossible to master, the problem is in your head, not your hands. Driving these negative ideas from your mind will be tougher than driving the bad habits from your present technique. I know, I've been there myself and, once conquered, I've seen it in too many people for me to count. On the flip side, I've heard the following rewarding comments from pleased, even struggling, Brace experimenters:

"The Brace reminds me to swing properly."

"It almost forces me to swing correctly each time."

"I can really feel a difference."

"I don't even have to think about it."

"The extra power is terrific."

"It's kind of uncomfortable at first, but after a while it feels natural."

"My swing is the same every time. I'm like a machine!"

"It feels more natural than my two hander did."

"It's automatic."

"It takes getting used to, but I've been swinging wrong for so long, I'm not surprised."

"It looks a little weird, but not compared to my old backhand."

"I can really feel my shoulders getting involved, on both sides."

"Wow, It even helps my footwork."

"It really speeds up my backswing."

"This is going to take a while because I have a lot of bad habits."

"If it could force me to watch the ball every time, it would be perfect." (Oh, how I wish it did!)

In all fairness, I should give equal time to those derogatory comments I have heard from some students, those who found it difficult to get used to the Brace. And there is a lot to get used to. It can feel like an overhaul of your entire style. Your timing, wrist and shoulder action, even footwork are altered. Some have given up after only a few attempts.

Their comments could usually be summed up with the phrase, "It's too uncomfortable."

I have often used the illustration that it is like wearing a cast after a doctor has broken a bone and realigned it so it can heal properly. The Brace, like a plaster cast, is forcing the proper form. It is going to feel strange, even weird. You will get used to it. Please be patient. I have tried to assure those who quit using the Brace that it would eventually feel natural. Sometimes, they don't believe me. It's only for those who are willing to go through the difficult transformation phase, especially those who have become, for lack of a better term, 'intermediates'. For some, it's too much change too soon. I can't help you avoid the discomfort of dropping a bad habit and replacing it with a good one. That's your fight. All I can do is ask you to trust me and assure you that it is worth it.

This book is mostly about the Brace and its potential for you. All other advice contained in it is window dressing. You can get similar things from other teachers that may surpass these extra tips and work better for you. But nothing you apply to your game will compare to the Brace. I hope you put in the time and effort to discover that.

Pound for pound, the Brace is superior to one hand or two on either side, but no technique is as effective without proper footwork. Given the choice between a one handed backhand with perfect footwork/weight shift/timing, and a lazy, off balance 'Braced' shot, even I would prefer the former. Put the two together each time and you are unbeatable.

The secret to Tennis
May be this new swing.
But if you don't move your feet
You can't do a thing.

Chapter Nine

Trust the Brace

When I make an error (which is extremely rare, ha-ha) it is for one of three reasons, usually. Either I took my eye off the ball because I don't practice what I preach, or I timed the ball poorly (again, practicing what I preach), or my opponent hit a shot that was simply too good (no solution to that except being first to hit the winner). I usually have little control over the third reason, unless it was my shot that set him up for it, but at least I can eliminate the first two factors. I like those percentages. Their correction will also mean fewer opportunities for my opponent to hit those winning shots. It's all good.

The slice backhand groundstroke was not shown in photos, but is vital for service returns, approach shots and defensive strokes. Simply pull the backswing up higher than a topspin backhand, but lower than a volley backswing. Push down and through the ball just like the volley, but closer to level, for a consistent and accurate alternative that will balance your backhand repertoire perfectly.

The most underrated stroke, yet one of the most consistent, is the forehand slice groundstroke. Many don't ever use this because the popular use of the Western grip makes this shot obsolete. But one who uses the Continental or Eastern backhand grip for serves, volleys, low forehands and wide service returns will see how efficient the grip is, and how effective the forehand slice can be defensively and offensively. The slice forehand looks a lot like the volley with a lower and longer backswing, more wrist and shoulder action, and a more level swing.

Be careful not to force the Brace by trying too hard to improve. It's going to take time, but it's well worth the effort. It took at least a year for me to perfect the Brace Backhand, and several years after that to confidently adapt it to my forehand. Just relax and let it work properly to transform your strokes. Feel it, don't force it. Learn to accept the Brace without feeling self-conscious or strange. I felt strange for years using it on the forehand side. The most difficult step is the first one, trying it with an open mind, as one student said when shown the Brace, "I'm afraid to try it." Don't be afraid. It can only help.

The alternative Brace, actually the original hold, and my favorite, is called the Wrist-Wrap. (**See photograph N**) Try them both. They both work. Find your favorite.

The fingers and thumb oppose each other and wrap around the thin part of the forearm just above the wrist. This Brace is best suited for two-handers and baseliners who use topspin for most strokes and need less variety in their game. The Wrist-Wrap is inferior to the L-Bow Brace for volleying, but superior in some respects for groundstrokes. I like and use them both, often switching back and forth between points. Experiment with both styles and find the one that works best for you. The same instruction applies for the groundstrokes and volleys using the Wrist-Wrap Brace.

There is so much not covered in this volume on tennis. This is the foundation, upon which you can build your unique style and strokes, hopefully utilizing the Brace successfully. I wish you the best in your quest to be your best.

I eagerly look forward to the day when I can ride my bicycle down the street past a public tennis court and see two young players using my novel method and having a great time getting better and better, knowing there is no limit to their proficiency potential. I hope I can hear them counting to two over and over.

I also want the backhand to lose its stigma as the inferior stroke, always the weak side. I want to see an equalizing take place between the two strokes. The backhand has been called graceful, challenging, frustrating, and natural, but rarely easy. I want to change all that . . . forever.

Trust the Brace. Let it guide you in the proper technique and it will eliminate your hitting flaws while giving you undreamed of power and control.

Keep your eyes on the ball
And the Brace will do it all.

The End (for the book)
The Beginning (for the reader)

Photograph N . . . Wrist-Wrap Brace